International Labour Office
Central and Eastern European Team

Pension Reform in Central and Eastern Europe Volume 2

Restructuring of Public Pension Schemes:
Case Studies of the Czech Republic and Slovenia

Edited by Elaine Fultz

Copyright © International Labour Organization 2002
First published 2002

Publications of the International Labour Office enjoy copyright under Protocol 2 of the Universal Copyright Convention. Nevertheless, short excerpts from them may be reproduced without authorization, on condition that the source is indicated. For rights of reproduction or translation, application should be made to the Publications Bureau (Rights and Permissions), International Labour Office, CH-1211 Geneva 22, Switzerland. The International Labour Office welcomes such applications.

Libraries, institutions and other users registered in the United Kingdom with the Copyright Licensing Agency, 90 Tottenham Court Road, London W1T 4LP [Fax: (+44) (0)20 7631 5500; email: cla@cla.co.uk], in the United States with the Copyright Clearance Center, 222 Rosewood Drive, Danvers, MA 01923 [Fax: (+1) (978) 750 4470; email: info@copyright.com] or in other countries with associated Reproduction Rights Organizations, may make photocopies in accordance with the licences issued to them for this purpose.

Elaine Fultz (editor)
Pension Reform in Central and Eastern Europe - Volume 2
Restructuring with Public Pension Schemes: Case Studies of the Czech Republic and Slovenia
Budapest, International Labour Office, 2002

ISBN 92-2-112981-0

The designations employed in ILO publications, which are in conformity with United Nations practice, and the presentation of material therein do not imply the expression of any opinion whatsoever on the part of the International Labour Office concerning the legal status of any country, area or territory or of its authorities, or concerning the delimitation of its frontiers.
The responsibility for opinions expressed in signed articles, studies and other contributions rests solely with their authors, and publication does not constitute an endorsement by the International Labour Office of the opinions expressed in them.
Reference to names of firms and commercial products and processes does not imply their endorsement by the International Labour Office, and any failure to mention a particular firm, commercial product or process is not a sign of disapproval.

ILO publications can be obtained through major booksellers or ILO local offices in many countries, or direct from ILO Publications, International Labour Office, CH-1211 Geneva 22, Switzerland. Catalogues or lists of new publications are available free of charge from the above address, or by email: pubvente@ilo.org
Visit our website: www.ilo.org/publns

Printed in Hungary

Table of Contents

Foreword   7

Chapter 1 Introduction: Explaining Pension Reform   11
Katharina Müller
   References   14

Chapter 2 The Political Economy of Pension Reform in Slovenia   19
Tine Stanovnik
   1. The legacy: Old-age security before 1990   19
      1.1. Developments to the mid-1980s   19
      1.2. New concepts in the late 1980s   24
   2. Old-age security in transformation, 1990–2000   25
   3. Explaining post-socialist pension politics   39
      3.1. Developments in the early 1990s   39
      3.2. The White paper   45
      3.3. After the White paper – the demise of the mandatory second pillar   46
      3.4. Parametric reform and the voluntary second pillar   51
      3.5. Parallel developments – a new pension fund and the 'privatization gap'   53
      3.6. Public opinion polls   55
   4. The actors and their roles in the pension reform process   57
      4.1. Domestic actors   57
      4.2. External actors   62
      4.3. The actors and the reform stages   64
      4.4. Deliberative forums   67
   5. Conclusions   68
   Appendix A: Interviews   70
   Appendix B: References   71

Chapter 3 The Political Economy of Pension Reform in the Czech Republic   75
Martin Mácha
  1. The legacy: old-age security before 1990   75
  2. Old-age security in transformation: 1990–2000   78
    2.1. The public pension scheme   78
    2.2. The supplementary private pension scheme   84
    2.3. Latest developments and reform proposals   88
  3. Explaining post-socialistic pension policy   91
    3.1. The federal period of Czechoslovakia   91
    3.2. Moving towards in-depth transformation   94
    3.3. Approaching the economic crisis   97
    3.4. The social democratic government   99
    3.5. Prospects   101
  4. Stages of reform and the role of different players in the pension reform process   102
  5. Conclusions: problems and policy choices   109
  Appendix A: Background interviews with key reform figures   110
  Appendix B: References   110

Chapter 4 Between State and Market: Czech and Slovene Pension Reform in Comparison   113
Katharina Müller
  References   139

TABLES
The Political Economy of Pension Reform in Slovenia

Table 1	System dependency ratio, pension expenditures and replacement rates, 1970–1989	22
Table 2	Actual retirement age by gender, 1992–2000	26
Table 3	Active insured persons and pensioners, 1990–2000	27
Table 4	System dependency ratio, pension expenditures and replacement rates, 1990–2000	28
Table 5	Revenues and expenditures of the Institute for Pension and Disability Insurance (% of GDP)	29
Table 6	Population, population structure and old-age dependency ratio, 1953–2001, with projections up to 2020	30

Table of Contents

Foreword 7

Chapter 1 Introduction: Explaining Pension Reform 11
Katharina Müller
   References 14

Chapter 2 The Political Economy of Pension Reform in Slovenia 19
Tine Stanovnik
   1. The legacy: Old-age security before 1990 19
      1.1. Developments to the mid-1980s 19
      1.2. New concepts in the late 1980s 24
   2. Old-age security in transformation, 1990–2000 25
   3. Explaining post-socialist pension politics 39
      3.1. Developments in the early 1990s 39
      3.2. The White paper 45
      3.3. After the White paper – the demise of the mandatory second pillar 46
      3.4. Parametric reform and the voluntary second pillar 51
      3.5. Parallel developments – a new pension fund and the 'privatization gap' 53
      3.6. Public opinion polls 55
   4. The actors and their roles in the pension reform process 57
      4.1. Domestic actors 57
      4.2. External actors 62
      4.3. The actors and the reform stages 64
      4.4. Deliberative forums 67
   5. Conclusions 68
   Appendix A: Interviews 70
   Appendix B: References 71

Chapter 3 The Political Economy of Pension Reform in the Czech Republic   75
Martin Mácha
    1. The legacy: old-age security before 1990   75
    2. Old-age security in transformation: 1990–2000   78
       2.1. The public pension scheme   78
       2.2. The supplementary private pension scheme   84
       2.3. Latest developments and reform proposals   88
    3. Explaining post-socialistic pension policy   91
       3.1. The federal period of Czechoslovakia   91
       3.2. Moving towards in-depth transformation   94
       3.3. Approaching the economic crisis   97
       3.4. The social democratic government   99
       3.5. Prospects   101
    4. Stages of reform and the role of different players in the pension reform process   102
    5. Conclusions: problems and policy choices   109
    Appendix A: Background interviews with key reform figures   110
    Appendix B: References   110

Chapter 4 Between State and Market: Czech and Slovene Pension Reform in Comparison   113
Katharina Müller
    References   139

TABLES
The Political Economy of Pension Reform in Slovenia

Table 1	System dependency ratio, pension expenditures and replacement rates, 1970–1989	22
Table 2	Actual retirement age by gender, 1992–2000	26
Table 3	Active insured persons and pensioners, 1990–2000	27
Table 4	System dependency ratio, pension expenditures and replacement rates, 1990–2000	28
Table 5	Revenues and expenditures of the Institute for Pension and Disability Insurance (% of GDP)	29
Table 6	Population, population structure and old-age dependency ratio, 1953–2001, with projections up to 2020	30

Table 7	Fiscal balance and public debt of Slovenia, 1992–2000 (% of GDP)	30
Table 8	Basic characteristics of the 1983, 1992 and 1999 PDIA (eligibility criteria and benefits)	32
Table 9	Pension funds and pension management companies: Accumulated premiums and membership (as of end of October 2001)	38
Table 10	Public opinion polls: 'What trade union organization do you trust most regarding pension reform?'	56

The Political Economy of Pension Reform in the Czech Republic

Table 1	Development of various pension system indicators 1960–80	77
Table 2	Development of various pension and macroeconomic indicators, 1993–2000	79
Table 3	Development of demographic ratios and system dependency, 1993–2000	80
Table 4	Old-age pension replacement rate for different wage levels	82
Table 5	Development of old-age pension levels, 1989–2000	83
Table 6	Development of nominal investment returns, 1995–2000	86
Table 7	Development of supplementary pension insurance, 1994–2000	87
Table 8	Demographic projections, 1995–2030	89
Table 9	Positions of political figures on pension reform proposals	108

Between State and Market: Czech and Slovene Pension Reform in Comparison

Table 1	Slovenia: Selected economic indicators, 1993–2000	115
Table 2	Czech Republic: Selected economic indicators, 1993–2000	117
Table 3	Selected demographic indicators, 1999–2015	119
Table 4	Basic features of the public pension schemes in the Czech Republic and Slovenia	123
Table 5	Basic features of the voluntary supplementary funds in the Czech Republic and Slovenia	124

CHARTS

Chart 1	Average portfolio of Czech pension funds	85
Chart 2	Development of transition costs after partial pension privatisation, 2000–30	91

Foreword

This is one of two volumes devoted to pension reform that are appearing as part of a series of studies of social security issues prepared by the ILO project, *Strengthening Social Security in Central and Eastern Europe through Research and Technical Cooperation,* sponsored by the French government. The research component of this project seeks to analyze the restructuring of social security schemes in selected countries of Central and Eastern Europe that has taken place since the political and economic transformation begun in 1989. The studies examine both social policy formation in the region's new multi-party democracies and their early experience in implementing reforms. The broad objective of the research is to provide countries still deliberating reforms with pertinent information on the recent experience and policy results of neighbors addressing similar issues. It is intended as well to empower the government's social partners in their role as participants in making social policy.

The research component of the project focuses predominantly on old age pensions. Other topics are also examined, however, and further volumes will address disability pension reform, the impact of social security reforms on gender issues, and the efficacy of social security reforms in combating social exclusion arising in the wake of the economic transformation. These studies will appear in the spring and summer of 2002.

The two pension volumes (of which this is the second) examine approaches to reform taken by four advanced EU-applicant countries, the Czech Republic, Hungary, Poland, and Slovenia. Hungary and Poland, on the one hand, have enacted major pension reforms that involve privatization of their national pension schemes, replacing them in part with systems of private, individual savings accounts managed commercially. In the Czech Republic and Slovenia, by contrast, governments have decided to reform their existing public pay-as-you-go systems without privatization. At the same time, they enacted laws that encourage citizens to save for retirement in private pension funds on a voluntary basis. Thus, the two volumes examine distinct policy choices made in a similar regional context.

The questions of key interest in the first volume bear on the early challenges of implementing the new privatization laws together with their impact on the pre-existing public pension system and on the adequacy of future pension benefits. Since Hungary and Poland are the most advanced CEE countries in pension privatization, their early experience in this regard is of considerable relevance to neighboring countries and provides an important opportunity for sharing knowledge within the region. The central focus of the present volume, by contrast, is on explaining the policy choice made by the Slovene government in favor of restructuring public pensions without privatization and, in the case the Czech Republic, the government's rejection of privatization and continuing search for consensus on public reforms. Given the broad interest in privatization in Central and Eastern Europe and the support for it by international financial organizations that provide many countries with development capital, we ask, why have these governments declined to privatize, instead seeking to restructure and strengthen their existing public, pay-as-you-go pension schemes?

The study takes a political economy approach to this question, examining the interplay of political and economic variables as they impinged on pension policy making in the two countries. It identifies several common explanatory factors including (1) the presence of well-placed actors in both reform debates with serious concerns about the high financial costs of the transition from pay-as-you-go to pre-funded pensions; (2) governments compelled to engage in broad consensus building by their coalition status (Slovenia) or by a succession of minority governments (the Czech Republic); (3) opposition from trade unions that were mobilized by what they saw in privatization as a threat to the future financial strength of the public pension system; (4) strong national orientations toward the European mainstream, reinforced by the presence of EU-sponsored programs like Phare in the area of pension restructuring; and (5) relatively low levels of external debt, which may have rendered these countries less open to influence from international financial organizations favoring privatization strategies.

The present volume contains contributions from three authors: Tine Stanovnik, professor of the Faculty of Economics and Institute for Economic Research in Ljubljana, developed the case study of the Slovene reform (chapter 2).

Dr. Martin Macha, former Director of the Research Institute of the Czech Ministry of Labour and Social Affairs and currently of William Mercer Associates in Prague, analyzed reform in the Czech Republic (chapter 3). Dr. Katharina Müller of European University Viadrina, Frankfurt (Oder) gave the research its fundamental shape, provided important counsel in the writing of the case studies, and contributed the introduction (chapter 1) and the conclusion (chapter 4), which provides a comparative analysis of the reforms. At the ILO, Markus Ruck provided a final critical review of the studies and Mercedes Birck implemented the final changes. We express our appreciation to the entire team and thank the authors for their excellent work.

ILO CEET gratefully acknowledges the support of the Ministry of Employment and Solidarity of the Government of France. We appreciate its understanding of the significance of social security for social cohesion and its commitment to support the strengthening of social security in Central and Eastern Europe.

We at ILO CEET hope that, by casting light on the dynamics of pension policy in two countries that have made unusual choices in a regional context, these studies will serve as a reminder that there is no single model for effective pension restructuring. Rather, there appears to be room for diversity aimed at matching pension restructuring to national conditions, needs, and values even in the difficult context of economic and political transformation.

Jean-Pierre Laviec	*Elaine Fultz*
Director	Senior Specialist in Social Security
ILO Budapest	ILO Budapest

Chapter 1
Introduction: Explaining Pension Reform

Katharina Müller[1]

Social policy experts have long been divided about the optimal features of old-age security, and more recently about the strengths and weaknesses of the two alternative financing methods.[2] Pay-as-you-go (PAYG) financing implies that current outlays on pension benefits are paid out of current revenues from pension contributions, thus calling for inter-generational solidarity as a necessary precondition. Contrary to this, in fully-funded schemes with individual accounts for workers, contributions are accumulated and invested over the entire working life, and retirement benefits are closely linked to the resulting individual balance.

Besides the much-discussed choice of the financing method, there are other design features of old-age security schemes that determine their economic and social impact, while reflecting the underlying social contract. Pension schemes can be publicly or privately managed, membership may be mandatory or voluntary, and there are defined benefit and defined contribution plans. While some retirement pension schemes are mainly designed to allow for a smoothing of individual income over the life cycle, thus stressing the insurance aspect, others aim to provide adequate retirement incomes for all, implying considerable redistribution. Coverage of the existing old-age security schemes can be linked to citizenship, to the place of residence or to dependent employment.

When debating the most suitable design of a pension scheme, opponents are usually divided by fundamental normative differences regarding the appropriate roles and responsibilities of the individual, the market and the state in social security, as well as underlying notions of social justice. This is also true for the

---

[1] European University Viadrina, Frankfurt (Oder)

[2] A concise summary and discussion of the arguments raised can be found in Barr (1998) and (2000). For an ILO view see Gillion (2000) and Gillion et al. (2000).

recent international controversy that was triggered by demographic ageing, financially troubled public pension schemes and, last but not least, a novel wave of radical reforms in Latin America (see Mesa-Lago, 1999; Müller, 2000). While the advocates of pension privatisation point to the iconoclastic Chilean reform of 1981 as a model to be followed, their opponents maintain that public PAYG systems should continue to be the main providers of old-age security, even though their technical parameters will need to be adjusted. The current pension reform panorama in the post-socialist states reflects this controversy to a considerable extent.

In the past decade, the countries of Eastern Europe and the Former Soviet Union witnessed not only a fundamental transformation of their societies and economies, but also of their retirement schemes (see Fultz and Ruck, 2000; Müller, 2002). This study focuses on the cases of the Czech Republic and Slovenia, two of the most advanced transition countries, where policymakers dismissed the privatisation of old-age security. Instead, they decided to improve the financial health of the public pension insurance with a series of parametric reforms, while complementing it with a voluntary private tier. This policy choice is in marked contrast with contemporary moves in several other post-socialist countries. In recent years, reforms implying full or partial pension privatisation were started in Kazakhstan (1998), Hungary (1998), Poland (1999) and Latvia (2001), while Bulgaria, Croatia, Estonia and Macedonia have enacted similar reforms and are expected to implement them in 2002. Other transition countries, such as Armenia, Georgia, Lithuania, Mongolia, Romania, Russia, Slovakia and Ukraine, are considering this type of reform for the future. These radical reforms coincided with the emergence of a 'new pension orthodoxy' (Lo Vuolo, 1996: 692) – a global epistemic community particularly active in developing and transformation countries, advocating the privatisation of old-age security (see Müller, 2001).

This collective research effort seeks to explain the observable policy outcomes in Czech and Slovene old-age security as a result of the interplay of economic and political variables. By so doing it intends to contribute to a multi-disciplinary strand of literature that has developed over the past few years. Recent studies on the political economy of pension reform in Latin America include Kay (1998, 1999), Madrid (1999, 2002), Mesa-Lago (1999), Mora (1999), Busquets (2000), Huber and Stephens (2000), and Mesa-Lago and Müller (2002). The making of pension reform in post-socialist countries has been analysed by Müller (1999), Cain (2000), Cashu (2000a, b), Orenstein (2000), and Nelson (2001). Brooks

(1998, 2001), Madrid (1998, 2001), Chłoń and Mora (2001), James and Brooks (2001), Müller (2001), and Orenstein (2001) seek to provide a cross-regional explanatory framework.

These analyses, that focus mostly on the explanation of the recent waves of pension privatisation in Latin America and Eastern Europe, were written in response to a bias in earlier research, that is limited both in terms of the geographical scope and of the types of reforms analysed. In spite of their differences in methodology and theoretical objectives, most contributions by economists, political scientists and sociologists show one interesting similarity: due to their exclusive focus on Western industrialised countries, they seek to explain the expansion of the welfare state, the remarkable resistance of social security arrangements to substantial downward adjustments, or the political feasibility of moderate retrenchment (for an overview see Müller, 1999). The authors claim that 'pay-as-you-go schemes may face incremental cutbacks and adjustments, but they are highly resistant to radical reform' (Pierson, 1998: 553).[3]

While these conventional approaches pay no attention to radical pension reform, spreading from Chile to other Latin American and East European countries since the early 1990s, the newly emerging multi-disciplinary literature on the political economy of pension reform risks focusing too exclusively on the full or partial privatisation of old-age security. Sure enough, half of all Latin American countries have embarked on partial pension privatisation by now, and so has one out of two post-socialist Accession Candidates to the European Union. Ultimately, however, research on the political economy of pension reform will need to take the full range of policy choices into account.[4] Notably in Eastern Europe, many countries still rely on their public PAYG scheme as the only provider of mandatory old-age insurance. Some of them have introduced substantial parametric reforms, yet relatively little effort has been made to explain their policy choice – against the recommendations of the 'new pension orthodoxy' and in favour of a more moderate approach to pension reform. So far,

---

[3] In a recent contribution World Bank-style pension privatisation is mentioned, but only in passing (see Myles and Pierson, 2001).

[4] In this context, it is interesting to note that in the 'new pension orthodoxy's' terminology, only pension *privatisation* is considered to deserve the label 'reform', or 'real reform' (see e.g. Browning, 1983; Sachs and Warner, 1996; Góra and Rutkowski, 1998), while less radical approaches are viewed as mere 'patching up' (Feldstein, 1996; Börsch-Supan, 1998).

only the studies by Müller (1999) and Cashu (2000a, b) have explored the political logic of parametric reform in post-socialist countries.

It is to shed more light on the cases where radical pension reform has been rejected, that we have decided to analyse the policy outcomes in Czech Republic and Slovenia. In the following two chapters, the individual country cases are discussed in detail by Martin Mácha and Tine Stanovnik, respectively. Both case studies are oriented along similar lines, starting with a brief summary of pension policy in the decades before 1990. They then proceed to give an account of the post-socialist transformation of old-age security, covering the period 1990–2000. The centre-piece of each case study consists of a section explaining post-socialist pension politics, with a separate discussion of the relevant actors and their role in the pension reform process. The concluding chapter, written by myself, compares the Czech and Slovene policy choices in the area of old-age security, starting with their pre-war and socialist legacy. Then the political, economic and demographic context and the pension reform measures that occurred during the past decade are reviewed in greater detail. Subsequently, this section seeks to come up with an comparative explanation of the paradigm choice of Czech and Slovene policymakers against the policy recommendations of the 'new pension orthodoxy'. The analysis is inspired by actor-centred institutionalism, while also drawing on the recent literature on the political economy of policy reform.

References

Barr, Nicholas (2000): Reforming Pensions: Myths, Truths, and Policy Choices. IMF Working Paper WP/007139, Washington, DC: IMF.

Barr, Nicholas (1998): The Economics of the Welfare State. Oxford University Press: Oxford.

Börsch-Supan, Axel (1998): Germany: A Social Security System on the Verge of Collapse. In: Siebert, Horst (ed.): Redesigning Social Security. Tübingen: Mohr, 129–159.

Brooks, Sarah (1998): Social Protection in a Global Economy: The Case of Pension Reform in Latin America. Duke University, mimeo.

Brooks, Sarah (2001): The diffusion of pension privatization over time and space. Paper prepared for the 2001 Annual Meeting of the American Political Science Association, San Francisco CA, August 30 – September 2, 2001.

Browning, Edgar K. (1983): 'The Economic and Politics of the Emergence of Social Security': A Comment, *The Cato Journal*, 3 (2), 381–384.

Busquets, José Miguel (2001): Las reformas de la Seguridad Social en Argentina, Bolivia, Chile y Uruguay (1981–1995). Paper prepared for the 2001 Meeting of the Latin American Studies Association, Washington DC, September 6–8, 2001.

Cain, Michael J. G. (2000): Globalising Tendencies in Public Policy, *EMERGO*, 7 (2), 6–19.

Cashu, Ilean (2000a): The New Politics of Pension Retrenchment in Russia. Paper prepared for the 2000 National Convention of the American Association for the Advancement of Slavic Studies, Denver CO, November 9–12, 2000.

Cashu, Ilean (2000b): The Politics and Policy Trade-offs of Reforming the Public Pension System in Post-communist Moldova, *Europe-Asia Studies*, 52 (4), 741–757.

Chłoń, Agnieszka/Mora, Marek (2001): Pension reforms: What stays behind them? Paper prepared for the joint IIASA World Bank Workshop on 'The Political Economy of Pension Reform', Laxenburg, 5 April 2001.

Feldstein, Martin (1996): The Missing Piece in Policy Analysis: Social Security Reform, *American Economic Review – Papers and Proceedings*, 86 (2), 1–14.

Fultz, Elaine/Ruck, Markus (2000): Pension Reform in Central and Eastern Europe: An Update on the Restructuring of National Pension Schemes in Selected Countries. ILO-CEET Report No. 25. Budapest: ILO-CEET.

Gillion, Colin (2000): The development and reform of social security pensions: The approach of the International Labour Office, *International Social Security Review*, 53 (1), 35–63.

Gillion, Colin/Turner, John/Bailey, Clive/Latulippe, Denis (eds) (2000): Social Security Pensions. Development and Reform. Geneva: ILO.

Góra, Marek/Rutkowski, Michał (1998): The Quest for Pension Reform: Poland's Security through Diversity. Warsaw: Office of the Government Plenipotentiary for Social Security Reform.

Holzmann, Robert (1994): Funded and Private Pensions for Eastern European Countries in Transition? *Revista de Análisis Económico*, 9 (1), 183–210.

Huber, Evelyne/Stephens, John D. (2000): The Political Economy of Pension Reform: Latin America in Comparative Perspective. UNRISD Occasional Paper 7, Geneva: UNRISD.

James, Estelle/Brooks, Sarah (2001): The Political Economy of Structural Pension

Reform. In: Holzmann, Robert/Stiglitz, Joseph E. (eds): New Ideas about Old Age Security. Toward Sustainable Pension Systems in the 21st Century. Washington, DC: The World Bank, 133–170.

Kay, Stephen J. (1998): Politics and Social Security Reform in the Southern Cone and Brazil. PhD Dissertation, University of California at Los Angeles, mimeo.

Kay, Stephen J. (1999): Unexpected Privatizations. Politics and Social Security Reforms in the Southern Cone, *Comparative Politics*, 31 (4), 403–422.

Lo Vuolo, Rubén M. (1996): Reformas previsionales en América Latina: el caso argentino, *Comercio Exterior*, 46 (9), 692–702.

Madrid, Raúl (1998): The Determinants of Pension Reform Around the World, 1992–97. Paper prepared for the 1998 Annual Meeting of the American Political Science Association, Boston MA, September 3–6, 1998.

Madrid, Raúl (1999): The New Logic of Social Security Reform: Politics and Pension Privatization in Latin America. PhD Dissertation, Stanford University, mimeo.

Madrid, Raúl (2001): Retiring the State: The Politics of Pension Privatization. Book manuscript, University of Texas at Austin, mimeo.

Madrid, Raúl (2002): The Politics (and Economics) of Pension Privatization in Latin America, forthcoming in: *Latin American Research Review*, 37 (2), Spring 2002.

Mesa-Lago, Carmelo (1999): Política y reforma de la seguridad social en América Latina, *Nueva Sociedad* (160), Marzo-Abril 1999, 133–150.

Mesa-Lago, Carmelo/Müller, Katharina (2002): The Politics of Pension Reform in Latin America, forthcoming in: *Journal of Latin American Studies*.

Mora, Marek (1999): The Political Economy of Pension Reforms: The Case of Latin America. Washington DC, mimeo.

Müller, Katharina (1999): The Political Economy of Pension Reform in Central-Eastern Europe. Cheltenham & Northampton MA: Edward Elgar.

Müller, Katharina (2000): Pension Privatization in Latin America, *Journal of International Development*, 12, 2000, 507–518.

Müller, Katharina (2001): The Making of Pension Privatisation in Latin America and Eastern Europe – A Cross-Regional Comparison. Paper presented at the joint IIASA World Bank Workshop on 'The Political Economy of Pension Reform', Laxenburg, 5 April 2001.

Müller, Katharina (2002): Pension Reform Paths in Central-Eastern Europe and the Former Soviet Union, forthcoming in: *Social Policy and Administration*, 36 (2).

Myles, John/Pierson, Paul (2001): The Comparative Political Economy of Pension Reform. In: Pierson, Paul (ed.): The New Politics of the Welfare State. Oxford: Oxford University Press, 305–333.

Nelson, Joan M. (2001): The Politics of Pension and Health-Care Reforms in Hungary and Poland. In: Kornai, János/Haggard, Stephan/Kaufman, Robert R. (eds): Reforming the State. Fiscal and Welfare Reform in Post-Socialist Countries. Cambridge, UK: Cambridge University Press, 235–266.

Orenstein, Mitchell (2000): How Politics and Institutions Affect Pension Reform in Three Postcommunist Countries. World Bank Policy Research Working Paper 2310, Washington DC.

Orenstein, Mitchell (2001): Mapping the Diffusion of Pension Innovation. Paper prepared for the 2001 Annual Meeting of the American Political Science Association, San Francisco CA, August 30 – September 2, 2001.

Pierson, Paul (1998): Irresistible forces, immovable objects: post-industrial welfare states confront permanent austerity, *Journal of European Public Policy*, 5 (4), 639–660.

Sachs, Jeffrey/Warner, Andrew M. (1996): Achieving Rapid Growth in the Transition Economies of Central Europe. Harvard Institute for International Development, Development Discussion Paper 544, Cambridge, MA.

Chapter 2
The Political Economy of Pension Reform in Slovenia

Tine Stanovnik[1]

1. The legacy: Old-age security before 1990

1.1. Developments to the mid-1980s

Social insurance in Slovenia has a long tradition, which is not surprising, since Slovenia was part of the Austro-Hungarian empire. The origins can be traced back to 1854, when the mining act introduced health insurance, accident insurance and insurance for old age. In 1858 railway workers were given health insurance, which was extended to accident insurance in 1869 and to insurance for old age in 1874. The first general scheme for health insurance was founded in 1889, thus closely following developments in vanguard Germany and Austria. There were no general schemes for old-age insurance, but in addition to the schemes for miners and railway workers, a scheme for civil servants was introduced in 1906.

After World War I, Slovenia became a part of the Kingdom of the Serbs, Croats and Slovenes (later renamed the Kingdom of Yugoslavia). This was a very centralized state, and the constituent parts enjoyed little autonomy. In 1922, general health insurance and accident insurance were introduced – or reintroduced, in the case of Slovenia and parts of Croatia. The other parts of the kingdom did not have any forms of social insurance prior to World War I. A general scheme for old-age insurance was first introduced rather late, in 1937, although separate schemes for certain categories of workers were enacted soon after World War I, such as for civil servants, railway workers and miners. The pension fund for civil servants in Slovenia was particularly known for its

---

[1] Faculty of Economics and Institute for Economic Research, Ljubljana.

ambitious investments in real estate, and an illustrious building in Ljubljana – the Skyscraper *(Nebotičnik)* – was wholly financed by this fund (Valant, 1978).[2]

After World War II, the social security system in Yugoslavia underwent fundamental change. The real assets of the former pension funds were mostly nationalized, and only a small share was transferred to the newly formed institutions for social insurance. In addition, the system was transformed into a pay-as-you-go (PAYG) system. Early post-war legislation introduced in 1947 contained certain Soviet-style features, such as different pensionable ages for various labour categories.[3] In organization and financing, the post-war social security system was in a state of flux. Originally decentralized and contribution financed, the system became strongly centralized by 1950, and was financed through the Yugoslav federal government budget. Then in 1952, a Federal Insurance Institute was formed and contribution financing was restored. The first serious devolution of federal prerogatives occurred in 1953, when separate social insurance institutes were formed in the individual Yugoslav republics. Although these had their own financial resources, they were still limited in autonomy, since the contribution rate was set at the federal level. The devolution process continued in 1955, when separate funds for health insurance, unemployment insurance, and pension and disability insurance were formed. A joint contribution rate was set at the republic level, and split into contribution rates to finance each branch of social security. Devolution also received a strong impetus with amendments to the Yugoslav constitution (and later a new federal constitution of 1974), enacting a vast increase in the autonomy of the republics and provinces. From then on, the general legislative pattern was for the Yugoslav

---

[2] This investment was subject to strong criticism, particularly by members of the fund, since the rate of return was supposedly quite low.

[3] These explicit provisions were not retained in later pension legislation, where special working conditions were taken into account, but in a more general framework and without specific reference to occupations. This was accomplished through the instrument of differing insurance periods and an earlier pensionable age based on working conditions. Thus, in later legislation an insurance period of 12 months could be counted as 18 months (or 14, 15, etc.). Of course, this entailed higher employer social security contributions. The insurance period was therefore increased by a given number of years, and simultaneously the pensionable age was decreased by the same number of years. A list of occupations entitled to the varying types of increased insurance periods (18 months for 12 months of insurance, and so on) was not part of pension legislation.

parliament to set broad guidelines or minimum standards in federal laws, with the republics given considerable latitude in formulating their own legal acts.

The early devolution and shifting of responsibility from the federation to the republics is a vivid feature of the decentralized nature of Yugoslav socialism. In the field of social protection, this system was characterized by a large number of institutions that assumed responsibility for social policy. These so-called 'self-managed communities of interest' were in fact bipartite councils, comprised of the relevant users and providers of social benefits and services. These groups would jointly decide on the level and quality of social provision (health care, pensions, etc) as well as the necessary contribution rate. In other words, they were given the power to tax, and this predictably resulted in very low transparency in public finances, with a myriad of taxes and contributions. True, the most important social security contribution rates, such as for health insurance or pension and disability insurance, were determined at the level of the republic (by the republic's own 'self-managed communities of interest'). But for certain areas of social policy, decision-making was even further diffused, down to the level of local communities. Thus, from the late 1970s until 1991, local actors had the right to set their own contribution rates for certain social services, such as childcare and social assistance. In spite of this general decentralization, the federation still retained some responsibilities in the area of social security, such as providing social security benefits to military personnel and pension benefits for World War II combatants.

The most important legal act on social policy in the 1980s was the 1982 Federal Act on Pension and Disability Insurance, soon complemented by corresponding laws at the republic level. The Slovene parliament passed its Pension and Disability Insurance Act (PDIA) in July 1983. The premise for the law was that pensions actually represent remuneration for active labour participation in the past. Consistent with this concept was a new pension indexation rule, according to which indexation was no longer based on the cost of living, but rather on wage growth.

The timing of the PDIA could not have been worse. In 1983, Yugoslavia plunged into a severe debt crisis, to be followed by a general political and economic crisis, which eventually led to the collapse of the Yugoslav federation in 1991. It is interesting that the authors of the 1982 federal act as well as its Slovene counterpart were not unaware of its financial consequences. Thus, these acts stipulated that the full application of the new pension indexation rule was to be postponed until the end of 1986. In fact, even a partial application of the rule resulted in a significant improvement of the relative income position of pensioners. As seen in Table 1, the replacement rate in 1985 was 66.5 percent, which increased to 74.2 percent in 1986 and 84.4 percent in 1987. The new indexation rule also introduced so-called back payments, compensating pensioners for the delay in adjustment.[4] This of course offered fine protection against inflation, which was already approaching 100 percent in 1985.

Table 1
System dependency ratio, pension expenditures and replacement rates, 1970–1989

	Insured persons per pensioner	Pension expenditure (% of GDP)	Replacement rate* (%)
1970	3.32	–	62.6
1975	3.51	–	67.8
1980	3.66	7.3	73.5
1985	2.94	6.8	66.5
1988	2.68	7.8	80.4
1989	2.52	8.7	80.0

* The replacement rate is the average net old-age pension divided by the average net wage. 'Net' is equal to 'gross' minus social security contributions and personal income tax.

Sources: For 1970, 1975 and 1980 Statistical unit of the Institute for Pension and Disability Insurance (IPDI). For other years, yearbooks of the social protection system of Slovenia. For GDP figures, *Statistical yearbook of Slovenia* – GDP figures through 1989 actually refer to 'social product', a narrower concept than GDP.

Though farmers had been under a separate pension insurance scheme since 1972, they were fully integrated into the general pension and disability insurance system through the 1983 PDIA. Even this separate scheme was strongly and explicitly subsidized by 'solidarity contributions' from employees, and this subsidization continued under the 1983 PDIA and other legislation (Košak,

---

[4] This delay occurred because wage data are available only with a two month lag. It was the application of back payments that was put 'on hold' until the end of 1986.

1996).[5] The 1983 PDIA also extended coverage to all categories of self-employed persons, again under favourable conditions.[6]

Under the 1983 PDIA, pensioning criteria were generous (see Table 8, which compares the law with later pension and disability insurance acts). The pensionable age was 60 for men and 55 for women, provided a 20-year pension qualifying period had been accumulated.[7] There was no age criterion for persons who had accumulated the full pension qualifying period, which was 40 years for men and 35 years for women. Conditions for early retirement were favourable, since they included only a required minimum age and minimum pension qualifying period. Deductions for early retirement were temporary – i.e. lifted when a person reached the age of 60 (men) or 55 (women). Accrual rates were high. The 1983 PDIA also significantly expanded the scope of various non-insurance benefits and solidarity measures. These included a pension income supplement for persons receiving low pensions, and a supplement for aid at home for pensioners with physical handicaps. It introduced new concepts such as the minimum pension and the minimum pension base.[8]

Although not all the 'goodies' in the bag were handed out – the new indexation rule was not applied in full – the relative position of pensioners improved markedly for two main reasons: generally falling real wages in the 1980s, and the determination of the pension base using a best-ten-year period of wages. One's pension could therefore be larger than the last salary or wage received. The very high replacement rates in this period can be observed in Table 1. The generosity of the pension system, as well as rapidly deteriorating economic conditions, resulted in a large increase in the number of pensioners and soaring pension expenditures.

---

[5] For farmers, the state pays the employers' portion of social security contributions. Farmers also have considerably more latitude in choosing their base for paying contributions.

[6] If a self-employed person was not insured prior to 1983, he could purchase years of insurance for all his past years of active occupation. The base for paying 'past' contributions was the average national wage in the year prior to the application.

[7] The pension qualifying period included the insurance period (i.e. the period for which contributions had been paid) and a special additional period (granted by law). This special additional period included, for example, years spent in the partisan resistance movement in World War II.

[8] If the computed pension base was lower than the minimum pension base, a person's pension was computed using the latter.

1.2. New concepts in the late 1980s

Slovenia was in many respects at the vanguard of Yugoslav republics. It was not only the country's most developed constituent republic, it was also a breeding ground for theories of social development and social experimentation. Even the concept of self-managed socialism was created by a Slovene, Edvard Kardelj, as a direct response to centralized, Soviet-type socialism. However, social experimentation went too far, and the Yugoslav system of self-managed, decentralized socialism eventually resulted in cumbersome decision making, non-transparent fiscal policies and lower economic efficiency.[9] By the mid-1980s social planners thought that the system had reached its limits, and that a greater role in society ought to be given to the individual. Their concern was not only with the individual worker in a self-managed enterprise, but also with the individual per se. Thus, the *Long-term plan of Slovenia for the period 1986–2000* stated that 'Socioeconomic development demands a change in some of the functions of the individual, the family and social institutions. While we will preserve and develop socially organized provision in the areas of health, education, childcare and cultural activities, we will nevertheless encourage the individuals' interest, responsibility and actions aimed at satisfying these needs' (p. 41).

Such general 'statements of intent' were further elaborated after the *de facto* demise of the self-managed system. Thus, an indicative planning document published in 1990, *The analysis of development opportunities for Slovenia: 1991–1995*, reiterated the 'new role of the individual, who is becoming more responsible for his health, education, social protection etc.' (p. 184). The analysis further suggested that 'mandatory insurance must be supplemented by various voluntary associations' (p. 210).

Freedom and the role and responsibility of the individual in society were not the only topics on the agenda. In the economic arena, discussions of the economic (in)efficiency of Yugoslav self-managed socialism were at the forefront of debate. At the heart of the efficiency problem was the concept of social property, which was a very distinct feature of the Yugoslav brand of socialism. Here, capital was not owned by the state, nor by workers, who were only 'managing' this property. It was owned by society at large. Of course, such weakly defined property rights

---

[9] The very decentralized structure in certain areas of social protection, such as child care and social assistance, has already been observed.

are hardly a recipe for the efficient allocation and use of capital. A privatization law, enacted in 1988, endeavoured to change this, mostly by providing a legal framework for management and employee buy-outs, through which social property would eventually be transformed into private property. Professor Ivan Ribnikar opposed this type of solution, and argued that in view of the genesis of this property, and taking efficiency and equity considerations into account, the *titulaire* ought to be someone outside the firm who would exercise passive ownership rights (Ribnikar 1989a, 1989b). Ideally, this would be a pension fund. Although very strong political interests prevented his proposal from being seriously considered, his ideas did influence certain developments in pension reform some ten years later.

2. Old-age security in transformation, 1990–2000

The first multiparty elections, held in spring 1990, brought to power a centre-right coalition government, and a referendum for Slovenian independence was passed in December 1990, with an overwhelming majority voting in favour. The Parliament of Slovenia formally declared independence in June 1991, and a new Constitution was adopted in December 1991. The new government was soon forced to intervene in the pension system, since the already high replacement rates were getting out of control. In November 1990, it introduced changes that modified the indexation rule, followed by a cap on pension expenditures in March 1991. The cap was not aimed at freezing pension expenditures, but at limiting the ratio between the average old-age pension and the average wage to 85 percent.[10] This measure immediately resulted in a large decrease in the replacement rate in 1991, though it could not prevent a further increase in pension expenditures, caused by a growing number of pensioners in the first years of transition (see Tables 3 and 4). This growth was due to a large increase in early retirement, which in turn was caused by enterprise restructuring and economic recession.

The new government also quickly introduced legislation on privatization and

---

[10] This ratio is computed by assuming that all actual old-age pensioners have a full pension qualifying period. This computed average old-age pension is then compared to actual wages.

denationalization. Through the 1991 Denationalization Act, the Institute for Pension and Disability Insurance (IPDI) recovered most of its predecessor's housing stock – some 6,500 housing units, of which a smaller portion was offered for sale to residents. The rest of the housing stock was to be managed by the newly formed Housing Fund of the IPDI. According to the 1992 Privatization Act, 10 percent of the value of social property of privatized firms was to be contributed for the initial capital of the IPDI's Capital Fund. Both the Housing Fund and the Capital Fund became separate and independent legal entities in 1996.

Preparations for a new pension and disability act started soon after the 1990 elections, and a new PDIA was passed by Parliament in March 1992. The 1992 PDIA reflects the profound influence of its 1983 predecessor. The similarity might appear surprising, given the turbulent period of economic, political and social change between the two acts, including the demise of the socialist self-managed system, the introduction of multiparty politics, independence, privatization and denationalization. The 1992 PDIA was not an ambitious or radical enterprise, but the government still hoped that the new law would contribute towards stabilizing the pension system. Eligibility conditions were somewhat tightened. A full pension qualifying period no longer sufficed to receive a pension – one also had to fulfil the age condition, which was gradually increased for men from 55.5 years in 1992 to 58 years in 1998, and for women from 50.5 years to 53 years (see Table 8). The age and pension qualifying periods for early retirement did not change, but additional strings were attached, for example, firm bankruptcy.

Overall, the 1992 PDIA may be characterized as 'too little, too late'. By the time the act was passed in March 1992, the worst in enterprise restructuring and downsizing was already over. Also, the tightening of statutory eligibility conditions did not prove a sufficient deterrent for retirement at the first possible opportunity. The practice of purchasing insurance years was widespread, since the price was low, with complete disregard for actuarial principles. As seen in Table 2, the actual retirement age increased only modestly, and was close to the statutory minimum age criterion.

Table 2
Actual retirement age by gender, 1992–2000

	Men	Women
1992	56.2	52.5
1993	56.2	53.3
1994	57.6	53.2
1995	57.5	53.1
1996	57.5	54.0
1997	58.3	54.9
1998	58.4	55.3
1999	58.2	54.8
2000	59.2	55.4

Source: Statistical unit of the IPDI, May 2001.

As seen from Tables 3 and 4, the number of active insured persons per pensioner (i.e. the inverse of the system dependency ratio) has remained stable since 1992. However, this is somewhat deceptive, because the stabilization was

Table 3
Active insured persons and pensioners, 1990–2000

	Active insured persons	All pensioners	Old-age pensioners
1990	884,600	384,100	197,300
1991	816,900	418,900	227,500
1992	764,900	448,800	252,400
1993	782,600	457,500	259,500
1994	772,500	458,100	260,800
1995	769,000	460,300	262,600
1996	765,700	463,300	265,300
1997	783,200	468,200	270,000
1998	784,200	472,400	274,500
1999	800,500	476,400	279,100
2000	807,100	482,200	284,800

Source: IPDI, annual reports.

achieved through legislative changes. Namely, the 1992 PDIA introduced several new categories of insured persons, among them (1) voluntary insured persons and (2) unemployed persons receiving unemployment benefits, for whom the National Employment Office pays contributions. In other words, the increase in the number of insured persons in 1993 was due to the introduction of 'marginal' new contributors into the system.

Legislative changes in 1992 were also partly responsible for a large increase in pension expenditures in that year, as the IPDI was required to pay health insurance on behalf of pensioners. This added at least one percentage point to pension expenditures as a percentage of GDP. After 1992, pension expenditures as a proportion of GDP seemed to stabilize, hovering at around 14 percent (see Table 4). This might seem to imply that the financial position of the IPDI has stabilized, but this is not the case. Until 1996, large increases in pension expenditures were matched by a continuous increase in contribution rates, and the overall pension contribution rate increased from 22.55 percent in 1989 to 31 percent in 1995, equally split between employee and employer contributions. In 1996, however, the

Table 4
System dependency ratio, pension expenditures and replacement rates, 1990–2000

	Insured persons per pensioner	Pension expenditure (% of GDP)	Replacement rate* (%)
1990	2.30	11.7	89.2
1991	1.95	10.9	73.8
1992	1.70	13.8	78.4
1993	1.71	14.1	74.5
1994	1.69	14.5	77.2
1995	1.67	14.7	77.9
1996	1.65	14.7	75.8
1997	1.67	14.9	75.4
1998	1.66	14.3	75.6
1999	1.68	14.4	76.8
2000	1.67	14.6	76.1

* The replacement rate is the average net old-age pension divided by the average net wage. 'Net' is equal to 'gross' minus social security contributions and personal income tax.

Source: IPDI, annual reports; White paper on pension reform; Bulletin of the Bank of Slovenia.

government decided to decrease employer contributions from 15.5 percent to 8.85 percent of gross wages, in hopes of increasing Slovenia's industrial competitiveness and preventing a downslide in labour-intensive industries. This marks a turning point – since 1996 the IPDI has become increasingly dependent on transfers from the central government budget (Table 5). Though government transfers to the IPDI were nothing new – the government had previously provided funds for various non-insurance benefits, such as favourable pensions in the police and military forces – the post-1996 transfers committed the government to co-financing insurance-type benefits, something it had not done in the past.

Table 5
Revenues and expenditures of the Institute for Pension and Disability Insurance (% of GDP)

	Revenues without transfers from state budget	Transfers from state budget	All expenditures
1991	12.7	0.2	10.9
1992	13.4	0.0	13.5
1993	14.0	0.5	14.1
1994	13.5	0.9	14.4
1995	13.0	1.1	14.7
1996	11.2	3.3	14.5
1997	10.9	3.2	14.4
1998	10.4	3.8	14.4
1999	10.1	4.0	14.4
2000	10.4	3.8	14.6

Note: Figures do not always add up. There were surpluses in the years 1991 and 1993 and mostly deficits in the other years.

Source: IPDI, annual reports and Statistical Yearbooks of Slovenia.

Following the passage of the 1992 PDIA, the government envisaged more fundamental changes. The main rationale was the worsening demographic structure of the Slovene population. Table 6 shows that the old-age dependency ratio (population aged 65 or over per population aged 15–64) has been continuously deteriorating for some forty years, and is expected to worsen in the period to 2020.

Table 6
Population, population structure and old-age dependency ratio, 1953–2001, with projections up to 2020

	1953	1961	1971	1981	1991	1999	2001	2011	2020
Population in millions, of which (age):	1.504	1.592	1.727	1.892	1.966	1.988	1.967	2.009	2.019
0–14	27.6%	27.3%	24.1%	23.0%	20.5%	16.1%	16.5%	16.4%	16.4%
15–64	64.8%	64.8%	65.6%	65.7%	68.5%	70.0%	69.4%	67.8%	64.7%
65+	7.6%	7.8%	10.1%	11.1%	11.0%	13.9%	14.1%	15.8%	18.9%
Old-age dependency ratio (65+/15–64)	0.117	0.120	0.154	0.169	0.161	0.199	0.203	0.233	0.292

Note: Figures for population structure do not always add up to 100, since for some persons age could not be ascertained.
Source: Statistical Yearbook of Slovenia for 1972, 1973, 1982, 1993 and 2000.

On the positive side, the fiscal balance of Slovenia was quite favourable, and certainly one of the best among Central European countries in transition. In spite of very severe fiscal pressures, particularly during the first years of transition, fiscal deficits were quite low. Public debt, while slowly creeping up, has not reached worrisome proportions, as can be seen in Table 7.

Table 7
Fiscal balance and public debt of Slovenia, 1992–2000 (% of GDP)

	Fiscal balance	Public debt
1992	1.2	–
1993	0.9	–
1994	0.0	–
1995	0.0	19.0
1996	0.3	22.7
1997	–1.2	23.2
1998	–0.8	23.7
1999	–0.6	24.5
2000	–1.4	25.1

Source: Ministry of Finance, *Bulletin of Public Finances* no. 3, March 2001. For GDP: *Bulletin of the Bank of Slovenia* (various issues) and for 1992 *Statistical Yearbook of Slovenia* 1994.

After the passage of the 1992 PDIA, some of the most glaring loopholes in the system were fixed in the ensuing years. In 1996, an option for so-called 'reduced pension rights' (for which lower contribution rates were applied) was all but abolished.[11] Also, the possibilities for self-employed persons to choose their own contribution base were severely limited.

The pension reform process started in 1996 and was formally completed with the passage of a new PDIA in December 1999 (this process is described in detail in section 3). The system was made rather complex, in no small part due to protracted negotiations within the government coalition, and even more between the government and the social partners. As an example of the system's complexity, consider the terms used to describe the relevant period for eligibility conditions. *Years of service* refer to the period when a person was actually insured. *Purchased period* is an insurance period that was purchased, either by the employer or the employee. *Insurance period* refers to the sum of the years of service and purchased period. *Special qualifying period* refers to years that are credited – such as those spent in the World War II partisan movement – and are thus included in the *pension qualifying period*. The pension qualifying period is the most important element in the calculation of the pension base, and includes years of service as well as any purchased period or special qualifying period. Finally, a *period assimilated to insurance periods* (or *added qualifying period*) is relevant only for achieving eligibility conditions, but not for the calculation of a pension. Such periods include years of university education, military service, and so on. These years can also be purchased, in which case they become a purchased period.

The reform embodied in the 1999 PDIA was concerned not only with changing the parameters of the first pillar, but also with the design of the second pillar and its supplementary pension schemes. The changes are summarized in Table 8. Again, one can observe path-dependency, since in spite of all the novelties, similarities to the 1992 PDIA are quite visible.

The 1999 PDIA introduced a number of elements that improved horizontal equity in the system. The gender divide regarding eligibility and benefits was considerably narrowed. Not only were accrual rates equalized, but the eligibility

---

[11] 'Reduced pension rights' means that the insured person is not entitled to all the rights offered by the pension and disability system – e.g. a pension income supplement, disability supplement, early retirement, aid at home or pension calculation from the minimum pension base.

Table 8
Basic characteristics of the 1983, 1992 and 1999 PDIA
(eligibility criteria and benefits)

1983 PDIA	1992 PDIA	1999 PDIA
Eligibility criteria		
Men: p.q.p. = 40 Women: p.q.p. = 35 Men: age = 60, p.q.p. = 20 Women: age = 55, p.q.p. = 20 Men: age = 65, ins.p. = 15 Women: age = 55, ins.p. = 15	Men:[1] age = 58, p.q.p. = 40 Women:[1] age = 53, p.q.p. = 35 Men:[1] age = 63, p.q.p. = 20 Women:[1] age = 58, p.q.p. = 20 Men: age = 65, ins.p. = 15 Women: age = 55, ins.p. = 15	Men: age = 58, p.q.p. = 40 Women:[2] age = 58, p.q.p. = 38 Men: age = 63, p.q.p. = 20 Women:[2] age = 61, p.q.p. = 20 Men: age = 65, ins.p. = 15 Women:[2] age = 63, ins.p. = 15
Minimum insurance period		
15 years	15 years	15 years
Pension base		
Best 10-year average of net wages[3]	Best 10-year average of net wages[3]	Best 18-year average of net wages[3]
Accrual rates		
Men: 35% of pension base for first 15 years, then 2% for each additional year, up to 40 years of p.q.p. Women: 40% of pension base for first 15 years, 3% for each additional year up to 20 years, then 2% for each additional year up to 35 years of p.q.p.	Men: 35% of pension base for first 15 years, then 2% for each additional year, up to 40 years of p.q.p. Women: 40% of pension base for first 15 years, 3% for each additional year up to 20 years, then 2% for each additional year up to 35 years of p.q.p.	Men: 35% of pension base for first 15 years, then 1.5% for each additional year of p.q.p. Women: 38% of pension base for first 15 years, then 1.5% for each additional year of p.q.p.
Pension indexation		
90% of growth of net wages	Growth of net wages	Growth of net wages
Minimum pension base		
65% of national net wage	64% of national net wage	Set nominally, but effectively at approx. 64% of national net wage
Maximum pension base		
350% of national net wage	310% of national net wage	4 times minimum pension base

Table 8 (continued)

1983 PDIA	1992 PDIA	1999 PDIA
Early retirement		
Men: age = 55, p.q.p. = 35 Women: age = 50, p.q.p. = 30	Men: age = 55, p.q.p. = 35 Women: age = 50, p.q.p. = 30 and other required conditions[4]	No special provisions, but certain categories of workers can obtain a pension without deductions for retirement before full pensionable age[5]
Deductions for early retirement		
1.5% for each 'missing' year till age 60 (men) or age 55 (women). 0.5% for each 'missing' year of insurance. Deductions temporary and lifted when age criteria fulfilled.	1% for each 'missing' year of insurance. Deductions temporary and lifted when age criteria fulfilled.	n.a.
Purchase of insurance period		
Generous conditions for farmers and the self-employed. In August 1990, possibility for purchasing years extended to certain categories of employees (firm bankruptcy, 'technological' redundancy etc.)	Employer can purchase (for employee) up to five years, under certain conditions.[6] Employee can purchase years of university education and military service.	Employer can purchase (for employee) up to five years, under certain conditions.[7] Employee can purchase years of university education and military service.

Abbreviations: p.q.p. = pension qualifying period; ins.p. = insurance period; n.a. = not applicable

Notes: (1) The increase in pensionable age under the 1992 PDIA was gradual, and was completed in 1998. All figures refer to final values. (2) The increase in the pensionable age and pension qualifying period for women is very gradual. Figures refer to the final values, which will in some cases be achieved in twenty years. (3) Indexed for inflation. (4) 'Other conditions' include bankruptcy of firm, disability, long-term unemployment. (5) Article 55, 1999 PDIA. (6) Article 214, 1992 PDIA. (7) Articles 195–199, 1999 PDIA.

Source: M. Štrovs (1984), J. Kuhelj (2000), and the 1983, 1992 and 1999 PDIAs.

criteria for women are now very close to those for men. While under the 1992 PDIA the earliest entrance into the pension system for a woman was at age 53 in case of a 35-year qualifying period, the 1999 PDIA increased the age criterion to

58 and the pension qualifying period to 38 years, only two years less than for men (see Table 8). Actuarial fairness is also more closely observed, since there are 'maluses' or penalties for retirement prior to (and bonuses for retirement after) the full pensionable age, which is 63 for men and 61 for women. The period for calculation of the pension base has now been extended to the best eighteen years, rather than the previous best ten-year period. Also, the act further diminished possibilities for the self-employed to 'tamper' with their contribution base.

Even greater emphasis was laid on the principle of vertical equity (or 'solidarity'). Thus, the ratio between two comparable pensions cannot exceed 4:1, a considerably narrower spread than the previous 4.8:1. (Comparable pensions exist when two pensioners enter the pension system under the same conditions and both have a pension qualifying period of 40 years, or 38 for women). A further redistributive element lies in the fact that social security contributions are not capped.

The main novelty in the first pillar under the 1999 PDIA was the introduction of flexible retirement, with maluses and bonuses. This quite resembles the Italian approach for flexible retirement. Retirement prior to the age of 63 for men and 61 for women entails penalties – although this is only a general rule, and not valid for certain groups of insured persons. Compared to the 1992 act, eligibility criteria were tightened, particularly for women, and benefit levels considerably reduced. Provided an insured person is not subject to maluses, his pension will be 72.5 percent of the pension base after 40 years of work, compared to 85 percent under the 1992 PDIA. Considering further that the pension base in the 1999 PDIA is the best 18-year average of wages (instead of the 10-year average according to the 1992 PDIA), the reduction in pensions is even greater. However, the new rules for eligibility and benefits are being introduced only gradually.

The 1999 PDIA opened the door wide for the development of supplementary schemes in a second pillar. True, a supplementary scheme was already introduced by the 1992 PDIA, and formed under the auspices of the IPDI. It was separately managed, and its assets were separated from other IPDI assets. There was never much life in this scheme, and its moribund character is seen in the number of its individual members, which never surpassed a few hundred.[12] The reasons for this were not so much the statist and monopolistic design features of the scheme, but rather a lack of tax incentives to participate in it.

The 1999 PDIA, as well as legislation preceding it, delegated a quite distinct

---

[12] By the end of 2000, there were only 739 individual contracts.

position to *Kapitalska družba*, the Pension Management Fund. This 100 percent state-owned institution has not only been given a very specific role within the second pillar, but was also given a strong supportive role for the first pillar. *Kapitalska družba* manages three different funds, which have been introduced through legal acts. First is the Capital mutual pension fund, the successor of the supplementary scheme introduced in 1992. Most of the original participants remained in the scheme, although some opted out and joined other schemes. Second, it manages a mandatory supplementary pension scheme introduced by the 1999 PDIA. This scheme covers insured persons in certain occupations, for whom employers are obliged to pay higher contributions in order to finance earlier retirement. This is not really novel, since even prior to the 1999 PDIA employers were obliged to pay higher contributions for employees in certain occupations, but previously these pensions were disbursed entirely from the first pillar. According to the 1999 PDIA, the employer is obliged to pay the 'normal' contribution to the first pillar (i.e. to the IPDI) and additional contributions to the mandatory supplementary pension scheme. These additional contributions are intended to provide the insured person with an occupational pension. Upon reaching the retirement age at 58, the person will be entitled to an old-age pension from the first pillar and a reduced occupational pension from the mandatory supplementary scheme.[13] The third function of *Kapitalska družba* is also stipulated by law – it manages the First Pension Fund, which was created to absorb ownership certificates given to the population in anticipation of privatization (see section 3.5.).

In addition to managing these three funds, the *Kapitalska družba* has a fourth function, which stems from the privatization act, in force since 1992. According to this act, the fund became owner of 10 percent of the social property which was to be privatized. The income from this capital was to provide financial support for the first pillar. In reality, it is financing the large deficits of the IPDI not only from its income, but also through sale of assets. In other words, it is being de-capitalized.

The conditions for the operation and management of collective and individual voluntary supplementary schemes are also detailed in the 1999 PDIA. It is assumed that larger employers will set up their own collective schemes, with

---

[13] Though not explicitly mentioned in the PDIA, this group of insured persons will certainly not be subject to penalties, although they will start enjoying their old-age pension prior to full pensionable age.

smaller employers joining in. The schemes must be approved by the Ministry of Labour, Family and Social Affairs and by the appropriate regulator (the Securities Market Agency or Insurance Supervision Agency). An individual can also join a supplementary scheme, though the tax incentive is less advantageous than the tax incentive for employers joining collective schemes.[14] These supplementary schemes may be operated as mutual pension funds, in which case the Securities Market Agency provides the necessary regulatory framework, or as pension management companies, in which case the Insurance Supervision Agency is responsible. Though there are no particular conditions regarding the portfolio structure for these pension schemes, there is a requirement for a guaranteed rate of return, which must not be less than 40 percent of the average annual interest rate on long-term government securities. There is also a requirement for the minimum number of members in a scheme.

Tax incentives for collective schemes are quite favourable, but they are conditional on a threshold of employees enrolled in the scheme. This was initially set at 66 percent of a given employer's workforce, but changes introduced in January 2002 decreased it to 51 percent. The initial threshold was somewhat problematic, since a large share of the workforce is either older or employed part time, and these employees are not particularly interested in contributing to such a scheme unless the employer is prepared 'to foot the bill' and pay all premiums. Employers are quite naturally reluctant to assume the whole burden, and usually demand that a certain share be paid out of wages. Experience so far indicates that employers cover more than 50 percent of the premium payments.

Employer contributions (premiums) to supplementary schemes are deductible for purposes of corporate income tax, social security contributions and personal income tax. Thus the tax treatment for these premiums is more favourable than that of other fringe benefits provided by the employer, which are subject to social security taxation and in part to personal income tax. On the other hand, employee premiums are paid out of wages and are deductible for purposes of personal income tax, but remain subject to social security taxation. There is a ceiling on the personal income tax deductions, which apply to amounts not greater than 24 percent of the individual's mandatory social security contribu-

---

[14] The 1999 PDIA actually did not distinguish between collective and individual supplementary schemes. Changes introduced in January 2002 require that a scheme be either collective or individual.

tions or an annual SIT 360,000 (SIT = Slovenian tolars), whichever is lower.[15] If employees regarded these premiums as a form of deferred wages, they would likely be more supportive of supplementary schemes – and as a result, trade unions would be able to exercise greater restraint when bargaining for wage increases. However, this is not yet the case. While employers regard pension premiums as an increase in labour costs, the trade unions fail to take a longer view of remuneration.

The number of pension funds and pension management companies has mushroomed, as seen in Table 9. It is too early to predict the future of this trend. In terms of coverage of the labour force, very much depends on whether employees in the public sector will join the supplementary pension schemes. Regarding the number of funds and companies offering pension schemes, it seems likely that some consolidation will occur.

---

[15] The nominal value was set in the 1999 PDIA, but it is subject to change. In January 2002 it amounted to an annual of some SIT 440,000.

Table 9
Pension funds and pension management companies:
Accumulated premiums and membership (as of end of October 2001)

Pension fund or pension management company	Accumulated premiums (SIT million)	Number of members
Zavarovalnica Triglav	1,287	27,230
Slovenica	42.6	3,164
Adriatic	22.5	1,345
KAD	766.6	5,919
Generali	18.4	2,507
Pokojninska družba SKB Banka Koper	45.9	>1,000
Prva pokojninska družba	247.4	11,195
Skupna pokojninska družba	825.6	8,500
Moja naložba	200.0	3,000
Krekova zavarovalnica	n.a.	n.a.
Druga Penzija	1.0	101
Pokojninska družba A	50.3	13,359
Abanka	n.a.	n.a.
Probanka	n.a.	n.a.

Note: 'Accumulated premiums' refer to the period up to June–July 2001. Apart from Zavarovalnica Triglav, all other funds and companies formally started operations in 2001. 'n.a' indicates 'not applicable' since the funds have not begun collecting premiums. KAD is the Capital mutual pension fund, managed by the state fund *Kapitalska družba*; it does not include the mandatory scheme, which is also managed by Kapitalska družba. The exchange rate in mid-October 2001 was SIT 243 / USD, or SIT 112 / DEM.

Source: Finance, 12 November 2001.

3. Explaining post-socialist pension politics

3.1. Developments in the early 1990s

Section 1 showed that fundamental changes to the social protection system were being seriously considered both from a practical and theoretical perspective already in the late 1980s, and concrete developments followed by February 1992. A new Act on Health Care and Health Insurance reaffirmed mandatory health insurance, while introducing a new voluntary health insurance. Though the act did not limit the number of providers of voluntary insurance, apart from the Institute for Health Insurance only one insurance company (Adriatic) applied for concessions. This insurance was mainly for co-payments, and it dampened the impact of reduced entitlements from mandatory insurance. For most insurance companies, the scheme did not appear to be a profitable venture, particularly since premium differentiation according to age, health conditions and other factors was not permitted. However, it proved to be an instant success, and most insured persons in the mandatory system immediately joined the voluntary scheme. In a similar arrangement, the 1992 PDIA introduced voluntary pension insurance under the auspices of the Institute for Pension and Disability Insurance. However, this is where the similarity ends. As already observed, the success of the voluntary health insurance scheme was not replicated by the voluntary pension scheme. Pensions from the first pillar were already very high, and insured persons were thus not really motivated to supplement this insurance with voluntary pension insurance. Also, contributions to voluntary pension insurance schemes were subject to social security taxation and (in effect) personal income taxation, which proved to be an important deterrent to participation.

Section 2 also noted the stark similarity between the 1992 and 1983 PDIAs. This similarity is not coincidental, since the 1992 PDIA was not an ambitious enterprise. Its main goal was to provide a comprehensive legal framework for pension and disability insurance within Slovenia's legal system. As shown in section 1, in the field of social protection the legal framework prior to independence was part Yugoslav, part Slovenian. Though legal acts of the former federation remained valid in many areas, the government felt that in the most important areas – including social protection – completely Slovenian legislation was a priority. This 'limited objective' attitude was unfortunate, since much more could have been done with regard to changing the parameters of the first pillar.

This is particularly true since relations among the social partners in the first years of independence were rather idyllic – one of the reasons being that the new trade unions were still in their formative stages. Nevertheless, the 1992 PDIA was even upon its inception regarded as temporary, and there was a clear understanding that a more fundamental shake-up of the system was necessary. This was to follow in some two years' time, policy makers believed. As a confirmation of the French proverb *le provisoire dure le plus longtemps*, these two years stretched into seven.

Following the 1992 PDIA there was some activity regarding pension reform, but with quite low intensity. Thus, in September 1994, the Ministry of Labour, Family and Social Affairs (MoLFSA) and the Institute for Macroeconomic Analyses and Development (IMAD)[16] jointly launched the project 'Reform of the Pension and Disability Insurance System', which was to be financed through the World Bank EFSAL facility (Enterprise and Financial Sector Adjustment Loan).[17] Although several foreign consultants were invited to submit tenders, the initiative proved to be a non-starter. According to officials of the Ministry of Finance, this project proposal simply could not qualify for EFSAL, as these loans were for enterprise and financial restructuring.

In October 1995, an IMF/WB team headed by the IMF's Peter Heller visited Slovenia, and shortly thereafter produced a report entitled *Republic of Slovenia: New challenges confronting the social insurance system*. The report presented a thorough analysis of the social insurance system, and in particular the problems facing the pension system. It strongly argued for pension reform, suggesting that it be performed in two stages. In the first stage, a parametric reform of the first pillar would remove the larger distortions and inconsistencies of the system, improving its financial viability and decreasing the size of the implicit debt. In the second stage, a multipillar system could be developed. 'The transition to a multipillar system would need to be gradual; indeed it would have to be, given the nascent stage of development of Slovenia's capital market', the report stated (IMF, 1995, p. 54). It is also worth noting that the report discusses various options for introducing a mandatory second pillar, but refrains from directly advocating or recommending its introduction. The report very strongly emphasizes the need to

---

[16] This institute is actually a government entity, assigned to monitor economic performance and provide macroeconomic projections to the government.

[17] This USD 80 million loan was disbursed in two instalments, in December 1994 and December 1995.

'address frontally the large outstanding implicit debt of the pension system' (IMF, 1995, p. 32). Of course, views on the importance of the implicit debt vary among experts. In the view of Giovanni Tamburi, 'the implicit debt is nothing more than an interesting sign post and a reference for setting social policy targets' (Tamburi, 1997, p. 15). Although this view has considerable merit, the size of the implicit debt nevertheless does give an indication of the long-term (un)sustainability of the pension system. Calculations performed by the IMF/WB team have shown the implicit debt of the pension system of Slovenia to be quite high, between 2 and 2.6 times annual GDP (IMF, 1995, p. 21). Compared to the G-7 countries, the implicit debt was higher only in Italy, and was comparable with Germany.

The IMF report produced a strong impact, not only by bringing more structure into the pension reform debate but also by its formulation of very concrete proposals for the reform of the first pillar. It gave strong impetus to the reform process. Soon after the report was published, a meeting of Slovene government officials and experts on social security was convened to discuss not only the IMF report, but also the draft outlines of the *White paper on pension reform* (November 1995). These were prepared by Giovanni Tamburi, Igor Tomeš and Dušan Kidrič following an international conference on pension reform held in Ljubljana in June 1995. The brief outlines were quite non-committal and non-specific regarding the choice of the pension reform path. Following this meeting, members of the working group for the preparation of the *White paper* were officially nominated in December 1995.

In January 1996 an unexpected political upheaval opened another window of opportunity. Namely, the United League of Social Democrats (ZLSD) stepped out of the ruling coalition, which at that time also included the Liberal Democrats (LDS) and Christian Diemocrats (SKD).[18] This proved to be a blessing in disguise, because following the parliamentary elections in 1992, the ZLSD was in charge of the MoLFSA. This reflected the party's preference to act as a guardian of social expenditures and prevent even the slightest attempt to reduce social rights. Such 'hyper-sensitiveness' to social policy is very difficult to reconcile with the need for fundamental pension reform, and after 1992 there were years of inactivity in this

---

[18] Following the December 1992 parliamentary elections, there were four parties in the ruling coalition – the Liberal Democrats (LDS), Christian Democrats (SKD), Social Democrats (SDS) and the United League of Social Democrats (ZLSD). By the end of the four-year term, there were only two parties left – the LDS and the SKD.

area. In January 1996, during preparations for the annual budget, the government proposed an indexation rule that was less favourable for pensioners, and also proposed a reduction of certain social expenditures (particularly on active employment measures). The ZLSD, outvoted at the cabinet meeting, indignantly withdrew from the coalition.

Tone Rop, a rising Liberal Democrat official and state secretary for privatization, was given the post of Minister of Labour, Family and Social Affairs.[19] This change brought extraordinary dynamism into the hitherto lethargic reform process. A policy paper on pension reform was produced in July 1996, entitled *Starting points for the reform of the pension and disability insurance system*, which was influenced by the 1994 World Bank publication *Averting the old-age crisis: Policies to protect the old and promote growth*. The policy paper was prepared by a 'core' working group, including Tone Rop as chairman. Its informal members were Miran Kalčič (IPDI), Marko Štrovs (MoLFSA), Dušan Kidrič (IMAD) and Milan Vodopivec (a former World Bank official and undersecretary at MoLFSA at the time).[20] The working group also included some other experts from the Faculty of Law, Institute for Economic Research, and the Central and Eastern European Privatization Network (CEEPN), which were assigned specific tasks in the preparation of the *Starting points* publication. In this sense the working group, whose members were actually appointed by the Minister of Labour, Family and Social Affairs, had a 'narrow' mandate and was unable to put all relevant pension reform options on the table.

The government acknowledged the *Starting points* in July 1996, and passed the document to parliament, where it was discussed in committees but never formally endorsed. This is because the report, while strongly advocating a multipillar approach, did not identify the defining characteristics of the new system. This policy paper came out clearly in favour of a mandatory fully funded second pillar. As for the first pillar, in spite of vague proposals and contradictory statements,[21] the document did suggest serious downsizing when it stated that 'in

---

[19] Mr Rop retained this post following the autumn 1996 parliamentary elections. After the autumn 2000 elections, he became Minister of Finance.

[20] Mr Vodopivec left MoLFSA in August 1996 to become dean and professor at the College for Entrepreneurship in Portorož. In September 1998, he rejoined the World Bank. He currently lives in Ljubljana and is a professor at the College of Entrepreneurship and consultant at the World Bank.

the first redistributive pillar of the new multipillar system, insured persons would acquire a minimum level of security for old-age' (*Starting points*, p. 86).

Parallel to the work on the *Starting points*, administrative preparations were also underway to include pension reform as a subject for foreign technical assistance through the Phare programme. This choice was not motivated by 'ideological' or similar considerations. It occurred because the Phare grant appeared at the right time and right place – the only other candidate for financing preparations for pension reform (a World Bank loan) was available only in May 1997. A French consortium, Quantix/Bernard Brunhes International was selected in July 1996, with Giovanni Tamburi and Pierre-Guillaume d'Herbais also joining the team.[22] According to the terms of reference, the output of the project was to be a *White paper on the reform of pension and disability insurance*, prepared in close collaboration with Slovenian experts. However, preparations for the *White paper* saw a slow start due to parliamentary elections in November 1996. The elections produced no clear majority, and after protracted negotiations a coalition government was finally formed in February 1997. The Liberal Democrats (LDS) led the government, and the Peoples's Party (SLS) and Pensioners' Party (Desus) were also members of the coalition. The key LDS ministers, including Tone Rop and the Minister of Finance, Mitja Gaspari, remained in place.

The Phare team first took stock of the work performed to that point by critically assessing the *Starting points*. Assessments by Giovanni Tamburi (Tamburi 1996 and 1997) and Pierre Mouton (Mouton 1997) were presented at a workshop held at MoLFSA in March 1997. They exposed the ambiguity and vagueness of the *Starting points*,[23] and endeavoured to bring more realism into

---

[21] E.g. on p. 54: 'The first pillar would preserve the existing features of social insurance... and it will fulfil two functions of the pension system: the insurance as well as redistributive function.' But on p. 86 we read: 'In the first, redistributive pillar of the new multipillar system...'

[22] Mr Tamburi was director of the social security department of the ILO in 1969–1989, and since 1990 has been a consultant at Watson Wyatt Ltd. He was extensively engaged in Phare and Consensus projects in Central and Eastern Europe, and also engaged in Latin America. Mr Pierre Guillame d'Herbais is a French expert on social security, and in 1995–1997 he was team leader for the TACIS programme of the EU, working on the reform of the social protection system in Kyrghizstan.

[23] It even exposed some pure nonsense, such as 'Pensions would be assessed... with respect to the level of professional education of the insured persons, taking into account a set of tariff categories' (*Starting points*: 77).

the pension debate – not only regarding reform of the first pillar, but even more so with regard to the introduction of a second pillar.

Mouton bluntly stated that the 'multi-pillar system to be set up in Slovenia, such as it is designed today, does not come close to the systems in force in the European Union'. With regard to first-pillar solutions, he suggested: 'Shouldn't we also eventually explore, in conjunction with an increase of the retirement age, yet another path, that is, that of flexible retirement?' (Mouton, 1997, p. 5–6). It seems that this latter suggestion did find its way into the proposals in the *White paper*. Tamburi carefully analysed the defining characteristics of the proposed second pillar, pointing out that 'the document does not suggest any specific rate of contribution' and further that 'finding a reasonable level of the contribution rate diverted to the second pillar is an urgent and difficult task' (Tamburi, 1996, p. 8–9). Tamburi also noted: 'The *Starting points* document does not develop the 'institutional' issue at all, although it will prove to be one of the most sensitive (politically, financially) aspects of the reform' (Tamburi, 1996, p. 10). With regard to financing the transition costs of reform, he wrote: 'The impression is that… (of an) over-optimistic assessment of the situation… It is unlikely that, in the near future, the State budget could allocate additional substantial funds for supporting the PAYG without sacrificing other areas of public expenditure which may have higher priority' (Tamburi, 1997, p. 12–13).

The final version of the *White paper* demonstrates that few of these early warnings and advice were heeded. The working group for the preparation of the *White paper* was headed by Tone Rop, and initially comprised mostly the same experts that were engaged in the preparation of the *Starting points*. These included a 'core' group of experts from the MoLFSA, IPDI and IMAD, as well as experts from academia and non-governmental institutions (e.g. CEEPN). A work plan with a precise distribution of tasks among experts was finally elaborated in May 1997, with the Phare team assuming responsibility for coordinating the task. The first draft of the *White paper* (draft version 0) was already produced by June. Thereafter, the working group was enlarged to include officials of the other two parties of the government coalition, the People's Party (SLS) and the Pensioners' Party (Desus), who attended the meetings in the role of 'watchdogs' to ensure that their pet-projects or issues of vital interest were included in the *White paper*. Their concerns and suspicions were not groundless, as their list was largely ignored in draft version 0. The SLS, catering to its rural electorate, was particularly eager to include a national pension, whereas Desus was keen to preserve the existing indexation rule which required indexing to net wages.²⁴ Desus also insisted on a legal obligation for the government to finance any future financial deficit of the Institute for Pension and Disability Insurance.

The *White paper* appeared in November 1997. The delay was somewhat unfortunate, since it was to have been presented at an international conference on pension reform issues throughout Europe and Slovenia, held in Ljubljana on 27–28 October. This conference, jointly financed by the Slovene government, Phare and the World Bank, was intended to give the strongest possible boost to the *White paper* and the proposed pension reform in Slovenia. It was attended by the World Bank 'top brass' in the area of pension reform: Robert Holzman, Michael Rutkowski, Roberto Rocha and Robert Palacios. Most of the papers advocated a multipillar approach, in which the second pillar would be mandatory and fully funded. This general approach was further elaborated by a number of papers that dealt with specific issues relevant for the design of the second pillar – such as institutional aspects, financial sector conditions, tax aspects and costs of transition.

3.2. The White paper

Although the *White paper* was not completed in time for the promotional and 'festive' international conference, it was soon given extensive coverage in the media and its proposals were analysed in detail. The *White paper* proposed a complete equalization of eligibility conditions and benefit calculations for men and women. The accrual rates it proposed were much lower than in the 1992 PDIA. It also introduced the term 'full pensionable age', which was set at 65 years. Persons retiring before 65 would have their pensions permanently reduced by a negative accrual of 3.6 percent per each 'missing' year, whereas persons retiring after 65 would receive an additional positive annual accrual of 6 percent. The *White paper*, as if inspired by the IMF study, proposed a rather short transition period, with final parameter values within the first pillar to be reached at a fairly quick pace.

In contrast to the very down-to-earth reform proposals for the first pillar, the proposals for the second pillar were quite vague. Thus, there was no explicit

---

²⁴ The devil is in the details – even the *White paper* states that 'the (indexation) rule is quite complex and difficult to understand' (p. 167).

mention of the contribution rate for the proposed mandatory fully funded schemes, i.e. what part of the overall rate should be diverted from the first pillar to the second. The simulation exercises on the macroeconomic impact of the second pillar assumed a rate of 6 percent, but this could not be regarded as an explicit proposal.[25] The simulation exercises show that under the assumption of a 6 percent diversion, the transition costs (the fiscal deficit and ensuing fiscal debt) would be quite serious. While the *White paper* does discuss possible means to finance the transition, this is more in the nature of a general discussion. On the other hand, the simulation exercises did have some good news to offer – the parametric reforms within the first pillar would produce a fiscal surplus in the medium term, by 2020, assuming the current contribution rate were earmarked for the first pillar only. After 2020, demographic conditions would worsen and the implicit debt would increase, though the scheme would still break even by 2050. The implicit debt for the period 1998–2020 was estimated at some 64 percent of GDP. These figures are not comparable to the IMF figures, as the assumptions on which these calculations are based are not explicitly stated.

3.3. After the White paper – the demise of the mandatory second pillar

Tone Rop was quite intent on maintaining high momentum and dynamism in the reform process. In order to strengthen his position in the coming months, he accepted the nomination for vice-president of the LDS (Liberal Democrats) and was elected to this post at the party congress in January 1998. In the same month, a tripartite negotiating working group was formed, comprised of experts from the MoLFSA, along with members of the trade unions and the employers' association. This working group was intended to streamline negotiations, as legislation on labour relations, labour remuneration and social security is usually discussed under auspices of the more elaborate Economic and Social Council (ESC). The ESC is not part of a formal institutional setting and was not created by any law, although its rules are set in government regulations. This is somewhat surprising in view of the power that it wields. As an unwritten rule, if the relevant legislation is not approved by the ESC, it is not 'ready' for Parliament. Officials of the MoLFSA soon discovered that selling pension reform to the trade unions was not

---

[25] Most experts assumed that the split between the first pillar and second pillar would be two thirds to one third. But in fact, this was never explicitly stated.

only a daunting task, but perhaps impossible. Initial optimism proved to be groundless, and the social partners refused even to consider the draft *Social Agreement on Pension Reform*, prepared in January. Moreover, the negotiating working group never discussed second pillar issues. As the trade unions declared themselves adamantly and irrevocably opposed to a mandatory second pillar immediately after the appearance of the *White paper*, it was deemed pointless to even discuss this subject. Negotiations were confined to the reform proposals for the first pillar, but even there, the negotiating group achieved little success.

The pension reform proposals did not receive an enthusiastic reception from academia either, and there too most criticism was focused on the mandatory, fully-funded second pillar. It is interesting that unlike in Poland and Hungary, where the mandatory second pillar was strongly supported by economists dealing with social security (Müller, 1999, p. 156), in Slovenia this support was weak and with many reservations. Even two members of the working group for the preparation of the *White paper* expressed reservations. Professor Tine Stanovnik from the Faculty of Economics pointed out that financing the transition 'will be an extremely difficult task for fiscal policy' due to the introduction of the mandatory second pillar (Stanovnik 1997). Professor Anjuta Bubnov-Škoberne from the Faculty of Law was harsher in her criticism: 'The introduction of the mandatory second pillar is highly debatable, and its social and economic effects very much open to doubt' (Bubnov-Škoberne 1998).[26] Though not explicitly referring to the *White paper*, Professor Ivan Ribnikar from the Faculty of Economics, a well-known expert on monetary economics and finance, summed up his position with regard to the mandatory second pillar – he was 'against it, or at least ambivalent' (Ribnikar, 1998 p. 474).

These initial expressions of reservation and doubt were followed by greater difficulties. The World Bank, in preparation for its Workshop on Second Pillar Issues held in Ljubljana on 23 March 1998, commissioned a paper from Velimir Bole, one of the most influential economists in Slovenia.[27] In his paper 'Financing the transition of the public pension system in Slovenia' he estimated the

---

[26] A particularly strong critic of the mandatory second pillar was Bojan Bugarič at the Faculty of Law. His article *Privatization of pension systems – an (in)secure strategy* (Bugarič, 1999) appeared after the demise of the mandatory second pillar.

[27] It is interesting to note that Mr Bole was not a member of the working group for the preparation of the *White paper*, even though he was invited to join it.

cumulative fiscal deficit due to the transition to a multipillar system (assuming an 8 percent contribution rate for the second pillar) at 74 percent of GDP till 2030 and 102 percent of GDP till 2050. In his second scenario, in which he assumed a pension system with only the first and third pillar,[28] the accumulated fiscal deficit is much smaller, 16 percent of GDP till 2030 and 25 percent of GDP till 2050. Of course, much depends on the assumptions, which were not clearly spelt out in the paper. Nevertheless, the message was clear – Mr Bole did not favour the introduction of the mandatory second pillar.[29] This seems to have decisively tipped the balance in the mind of the Minister of Finance, Mr Gaspari. At that very workshop, he declared that a mandatory second pillar would not be fiscally feasible.

The trade unions, which were quite uncooperative in the negotiating working group, decided to 'rub in' their message further. They organized several demonstrations, the largest of which was sponsored by the Free Trade Unions of Slovenia (FTUS) on 28 March, with some 10,000 participants. Under the slogan 'old-age security cannot be the privilege of the rich', strong opposition to the pension reform plan was voiced, particularly against the high pensionable age (65), gender equalization and the introduction of the mandatory second pillar. Dušan Semolič, president of the FTUS, exclaimed that the union was against the mandatory second pillar 'because it signifies the end of intergenerational solidarity, with dire consequences for low-income workers and the unemployed. The mandatory second pillar would be in the interests of the ruling political and financial elite and their thirst for money, profits and power' (*Dnevnik*, 30 March 1998).

At the same time, a mission of Slovene MPs and journalists visited Switzerland in a study and fact-finding mission on pension systems. MPs continued their trip to the Netherlands, and the journalists – lead by Tone Rop – visited Rome. Upon departure from Rome, a trade union leader presented Mr Rop with a gift: a video recording of the massive demonstrations against prime minister Silvio Berlusconi in 1994. These demonstrations compelled the government to renounce plans for pension reform, and eventually led to the fall of the Berlusconi government.

---

[28] A pension system for Slovenia with a first and third pillar had already been proposed by Stanovnik and Kukar (1994).

[29] Veljko Bole noted that he approached the problem of determining the size and dynamics of the fiscal deficit without any bias or preconceived opinion (for or against the mandatory second pillar). Roberto Rocha (World Bank) was aghast and bitterly disappointed after Bole's presentation, even more so since the World Bank financed his research. The World Bank's plan to publish the proceedings of the workshop was also cancelled (interview, Bole).

There is little doubt that this token had a strong impact on Mr Rop, and greatly diminished his resolve in pushing through pension reform against the wishes of the Slovenian trade unions (interview, Kanduti).

After this rapid succession of events, Mr Rop 'simply pulled the mandatory second pillar out of circulation' (interview, Gaspari). This seems to be an accurate description, since the decision was never discussed at cabinet meetings. The mandatory second pillar seems to have met its definitive demise at the cabinet meeting on 23 April, when the government proposed lower VAT rates than those originally envisaged for the draft law on VAT. Thus, a proposed one or two percentage points of VAT earmarked for financing the transition evaporated. At that very same cabinet meeting, the government issued a document entitled *Opinion of the Government of Slovenia regarding the position of the FTUS toward the White paper on pension reform*. In this document, the government expressed its strong disapproval with the view of the FTUS that 'the mandatory fully-funded second pillar is a risky strategy', but in the same breath proposes the gradual introduction of a voluntary fully-funded second pillar. The *Opinion* was actually prepared by Mr Rop's ministry and virtually rubber-stamped by the cabinet without discussion.[30] It is noteworthy that the government responded directly to the FTUS. This was an acknowledgment of the dominant role of the FTUS among trade unions and their role as *the* veto actor in the process. At the same meeting, the government also gave Mr Rop a continuing and full mandate for negotiations with the social partners.

To an outside observer, it might be difficult to grasp the extreme leeway given to Mr Rop, not only in conceiving pension reform, but also in the tactics used to achieve it. Part of the explanation can be ascribed to his position as second-in-command within the ruling party (LDS) hierarchy.[31] Also significant is the very way the Slovenian government functions, as ministers quite frequently assume full responsibility for carrying out particular projects.[32] The pension reform was

---

[30] There were some minor and completely irrelevant additions proposed by the vice prime minister, Marjan Podobnik, a member of the SLS.

[31] In contrast, the Minister of Finance, Mitja Gaspari, also a member of the LDS, was without any political function within the LDS (and probably also without any political ambitions).

[32] This view is also supported by a political analyst, Professor Vlado Miheljak, who describes the LDS not only as an extremely decentralized party, but one in which individualists predominate. 'That is why nobody in the party bothers about factions and dissenters; considering the inner dynamics of the party, these are meaningless terms' (Miheljak 2001).

Mr Rop's project, and it was his role to bring it to fruitful completion. In effect, he received an implicit mandate. It was his business to choose the appropriate tactics to achieve this mandate, and nobody in the government wanted to be bothered with progress reports. Even more, meddling into one's project is deeply resented and interpreted as hostile action. Thus, when later on in the reform process the prime minister, Janez Drnovšek, tried to intervene in order to resolve a negotiation deadlock by meeting the president of the FTUS, Mr Rop energetically prevented him from doing so.

In analysing the demise of the mandatory second pillar (which occurred, in the words of TS Eliot, 'not with a bang but with a whimper'), several causes can be pinpointed. A large part of the explanation can be traced to the design features of the mandatory second pillar, which were weak. Particularly worrisome was the lack of a clear blueprint for financing the transition caused by its introduction. The analysis of this very important issue in the *White paper* was quite vague, and not much changed in the following months. Of course, there was talk that VAT would absorb part of the burden, with one or two percentage points earmarked for transition. But it appears that there was never any serious discussion on how to finance the transition. In the words of Mr Gaspari, the Minister of Finance, Mr Rop simply did not want to discuss this question (interview, Gaspari). The important actors in pension reform quickly took note of this vagueness. Thus, Janko Kušar, the president of the Desus party, perceived that there was a persistent fear that the introduction of the mandatory second pillar would result in a large fiscal deficit, which would then quickly translate into serious pension reductions in the first pillar (interview, Kušar). This was the underlying reason that Desus, although a member of the ruling coalition, was opposed to the mandatory second pillar. This 'gut feeling' has a rational explanation. In terms of political economy, the introduction of the mandatory second pillar might imply a 'hidden agenda'. As a share of social security contributions is diverted to a mandatory second pillar, the fiscal sustainability of the first pillar could be undermined (Müller, 1999, p. 164).

It seems that a similar line of reasoning was also behind the opposition of the trade unions to the mandatory second pillar. They believed – like Desus – that the introduction of the mandatory second pillar would soon lead to a serious erosion of pensions in the first pillar. While the unions never expressed these reservations publicly, they probably explain their uncompromising position on the introduction of the mandatory second pillar. Why would someone strongly oppose the mandatory second pillar and enthusiastically support a voluntary second pillar – even demanding generous tax incentives for it? This somewhat schizophrenic attitude could only be explained by the concern about the impact of the mandatory second pillar on the pension benefits in the first pillar.

3.4. Parametric reform and the voluntary second pillar

After the momentous developments of April 1998, there was still a bumpy road ahead. At the fateful April cabinet meeting, Mr Rop also obtained a clear mandate to proceed with preparations on the draft law. As there was no progress in negotiations with the trade unions, this clever tactical manoeuvre – almost certainly conceived by Mr Rop himself – aimed to put pressure on them to be more cooperative in the pension reform process. On 30 July the government approved the draft Pension and Disability Insurance Act, which included most of the original proposals for parametric reform of the first pillar that had been enunciated in the *White paper*. The draft also contained the necessary legal framework for supplementary pension schemes in a voluntary second pillar.[33]

In July the negotiating working group, comprised of members of MoLFSA, trade unions and employers' associations, resumed its work under a new name – the coordinating working group. After protracted and tough negotiations, two social agreements were signed on 28 April 1999, one with the employers' associations and the other with the trade union organizations. These agreements stipulated the basic parameters for the first pillar, the transition period required for these changes, as well as the values of bonuses for retirement after (and maluses for retirement before) full pensionable age. The pensionable age was set at 63 for men and 61 for women. The agreement paved the way for a second and eventually a third reading of the law.

Though problems with the social partners were resolved, there still remained one contentious area. Namely, following the demise of the mandatory second pillar, Mr Rop was adamant that supplementary pension schemes be given the most favourable tax treatment. Apart from including a ceiling and a floor on the amount of premiums that qualify for favourable tax treatment, the draft law

---

[33] The draft law was written by the same group of core experts from the MoLFSA, IPDI and IMAD that were involved in the preparation of the *Starting points* and *White paper*. The large section on supplementary schemes was mostly written by Nina Plavšak from the Central Securities Clearing Corporation.

envisaged a 'pure' EET (exempt-exempt-taxed) treatment. In other words, the employers' premiums for supplementary schemes were to be exempted from all forms of taxes, including corporate income tax, (mandatory) social security contributions and personal income tax.[34] Senior officials from the Ministry of Finance were not opposed to favourable tax treatment in principle, but they thought that the tax treatment of premiums as envisaged in the draft law was 'too' favourable, as compared with other employer fringe benefits. Such benefits are subject not only to social security taxation in Slovenia, but also to personal income taxation under certain conditions.[35] These officials demanded that premiums be given the same tax treatment as other fringe benefits granted by the employer. In a shouting session in October 1999 in Mr Gaspari's office, Mr Bole, who was invited to the meeting, advocated this generous tax treatment. It seems that he tipped the balance once again.[36] Mr Rop, who regarded this issue as one of the cornerstones of pension reform, got his way.[37] He hoped that this 'soft', voluntary approach toward supplementary pension schemes through very strong tax incentives would eventually produce a result similar to the 'hard' approach – i.e. through a mandatory second pillar.[38]

The law was then sent to Parliament for a third reading, and was finally enacted on 23 December 1999, with 50 MPs voting for and 19 against. Of 456 articles, some 100 deal with supplementary schemes. One could argue that social security law does not have much in common with the regulation of mutual funds and pension management companies, but most experts agree that this 'bundling' was absolutely essential for the passage of the law and completion of the pension reform process. It was felt that the bitter pill of entitlement severance and benefit

---

[34] In contrast, employee contributions were to be exempted from personal income tax only.

[35] Interestingly enough, when calculating social security benefits, these fringe benefits are not taken into account in assessing the pension base.

[36] Mr Gaspari stated that he supported this very favourable tax treatment all along. One participant at the shouting session claimed that Mr Gaspari expressed his support following Mr Bole's argumentation.

[37] It might seem surprising that such an important issue was discussed toward the end of the legislative process. This is not uncommon, and vital discussions are frequently postponed till the very last moment.

[38] The ease with which Mr Rop abandoned the mandatory second pillar is nevertheless surprising, as is the fervour with which he advocated the 'exceptional' tax treatment of employer premiums for supplementary schemes.

reduction in the first pillar must be compensated by new voluntary saving opportunities in the second pillar. If it had been necessary to draft separate laws for the first and second pillars, the responsibility for drafting the second pillar law would have certainly gone to the Ministry of Finance. There is reason to believe that this ministry would have approached the task with less than full enthusiasm.

3.5. Parallel developments – a new pension fund and the 'privatization gap'

There were no alternate or competing proposals for pension reform that were comprehensive in scope. The actors involved all endeavoured to influence the mainstream agenda, which was in fact set by the Ministry of Labour, Family and Social Affairs. The trade unions, the Peoples' Party (SLS) and Pensioners' Party (Desus) did not have anything even resembling a comprehensive plan for pension reform. Their role was confined to influencing the reform process, particularly regarding changes in the first pillar.

There was but one important parallel development during the pension reform process, which could be regarded as a partial but complementary proposal for the formation of the second pillar. This proposal invoked an idea first put forward by Professor Ivan Ribnikar in 1989 (described in section 1), and further developed during the pension reform process (Ribnikar 1998). It was operationalized at the Ministry of Finance in 1998, with the strong approval of Mr Gaspari, who even became personally engaged in the formulation of the draft law.

Ribnikar's original proposal offered a possible solution for the Yugoslav (and Slovene) privatization problem, by placing all social assets into the hands of a pension fund or funds. This solution would, in a simple manner, circumvent the need for 'real' privatization, and would also have distinct advantages with regard to fairness. However, Slovenia undertook a different privatization model, and executed at a slow pace in a sloppy manner.[39] This form of privatization resulted in a mismatch between the (market) value of social assets that were to be privatized, and the value of ownership certificates given to the population. This difference was labelled the 'privatization gap', and was still a contentious issue at the time of pension reform. It was suggested that additional state property (which was never on the privatization agenda) be sold in order to transform all

---

[39] The privatization model that was adopted is rather complicated, as several privatization methods were permitted. The dominant method turned out to be the management-employee buyout. For more, see World Bank (1999).

ownership certificates into shares. The government was understandably very reluctant to give away state assets in this manner, and had thus been dragging its feet on the issue for several years.

Professor Ribnikar proposed in January 1998 that the 'privatization gap' simply represent government liabilities toward a 'new' pension fund. Persons who still had ownership certificates could then trade these in for a supplementary pension to be received from this fund. The advantage of such a solution would be that the government would not be under great pressure to match the liability toward this fund with real assets immediately, though it would nevertheless have a firm commitment to provide (within a reasonable time period) the necessary assets (financial or real) for the pension fund. The fund would be part of the second pillar.

The idea of finally solving the lingering privatization problem and at the same time contributing toward the pension reform was very appealing to Mr Gaspari. The 'authorized investment companies', a product of Slovenia's privatization model, were ceaselessly clamouring for the sale of state property in order to fill the privatization gap. Mr Gaspari, never a fervent supporter of these companies, regarded the 'new' pension fund as an ideal instrument for holding them at bay, while also providing an opportunity to set in place a strong constituent element of the second pillar.

With collaboration from the ubiquitous Mr Bole, a draft law on this pension fund was prepared at the Ministry of Finance. Nobody dared directly oppose the proposal outright, but strong lobbying by the authorized investment companies and the SLS succeeded in rendering the law quite ineffective. The SLS wanted to address the privatization gap through the use of government bonds, so they viewed Gaspari's proposal as contrary to their interests. The authorized investment companies viewed the new pension fund as a clever device to deprive them of state assets that were within their reach. The proposal was diluted and rendered ineffective in an ingenious way, by setting a limit on the number of pension coupons per person. Persons could swap their ownership certificates (or rather the remaining value of this certificate) into pension coupons of the new pension fund. They could even trade with these coupons, but because a limit of 10,000 coupons per person was imposed, they could at best manage to acquire quite a small supplementary pension. This limit was based on the populist argument that it would prevent speculators from trading and profiting. Just to be on the safe side, the SLS also succeeded in modifying the original proposal to swap ownership certificates for pension coupons. The original proposal was that this swap would be effective by default, but the final accepted procedure was the reverse: if a person wanted to swap ownership certificates for pension coupons, he would have to submit an explicit statement to that effect.

The law was finally passed by Parliament in June 1999. It did not make a serious dent in the privatization gap. Even extremely favourable tax treatment – in effect EEE (exempt-exempt-exempt) – could not alter the fate of this law. The new pension fund, named the First Pension Fund, managed to capture only some 5 percent of the total value of remaining ownership certificates, which were swapped for pension coupons. As has already been observed, this fund is managed by the state-owned *Kapitalska družba*.

3.6. Public opinion polls

Public opinion was closely monitored during the pension reform process, particularly in the final phase of negotiations with the social partners, from October 1998 to April 1999. In these polls a very large number of respondents (about 70 percent) expressed support for pension reform, but only some 10 percent said they had a good understanding of its basic features. Public support for the reform was slowly losing ground, probably as people became more informed and aware of its implications. While in November 1998 54 percent of the respondents supported the pension reform proposals, the support was decreasing continuously, reaching 45 percent in March 1999, when a full 81 percent of respondents were against the government proposal on the full pensionable age (65 for men, 63 for women). Meanwhile, 52 percent declared themselves in favour of a compromise value (63 for men, 61 for women), which was proposed by the ZLSD (United League of Social Democrats). The March 1999 opinion poll probably influenced Tone Rop in softening his position on the full pensionable age, which eventually led to the signing of the *Social Agreement on the Reform of Pension and Disability Insurance in Slovenia* in April 1999.

Public opinion polls also served to measure the popularity and support for the main actors in the pension reform process. The polls showed that the credibility and trustworthiness of Mr Rop and the trade unions were never very different in the mind of the public, and the percentage differences were certainly not statistically significant. With regard to the perceived credibility and trustworthiness of the various trade unions, the FTUS clearly came out on top, and this established them as the main social partner. The strong support for the FTUS can be observed in Table 10.

Table 10
Public opinion polls:
'What trade union organization do you trust most regarding pension reform?'

	November 1998	March 1999
Trade union organizations:		
– FTUS	32.2	30.2
– Pergam	2.9	4.7
– Confederation Independence	5.1	4.1
– Confederation 90	0.4	1.1
None of the above	34.3	18.4
All	–	3.8
Don't know, undecided	25.1	37.7

Source: Studio 3 S, public opinion polls, October 1998 – March 1999.

4. The actors and their roles in the pension reform process

The pension reform process in Slovenia is characterized by a small number of actual proposal and veto actors.

4.1. Domestic actors

Ministry of Labour, Family and Social Affairs

There is absolutely no doubt that the Minister of Labour, Family and Social Affairs, Tone Rop, was firmly in charge of the pension reform project. The Ministry's experts who were involved in the project were quite supportive of the original reform proposals. Though a Phare team acted as a strong coordinator, particularly in the early preparations of the *White paper* (draft version 0), the final version was very much a 'domestic' product, in which experts from the MoLFSA, IPDI and IMAD played the largest roles.

The energetic, tough and abrasive Tone Rop was wholly committed to steering the project to successful conclusion. However, when the *White paper* entered the political arena, and when difficulties in selling the reform mounted, Mr Rop assumed the role of political broker. We have observed the quick succession of events during March and April 1998, which caused the abandonment of the mandatory second pillar. Mr Rop ascribed this to the coinciding opposition of two unlikely bedfellows: the Ministry of Finance and the trade unions. This swift dismissal of one of the centrepieces of the pension reform appears surprising, but it nevertheless demonstrates the political instinct and pragmatism of Mr Rop.[40]

The government coalition

It would be quite naive to view the government coalition as a homogeneous team with a clear agenda. Following the 1996 elections, the coalition included the LDS (Liberal Democrats), the SLS (People's Party) and Desus (Pensioners' Party). In the 90-seat Parliament, these parties had a comfortable majority of 49 seats – 25 for the LDS, 19 for the SLS and 5 for Desus.[41] We have already observed that the government more resembled a group of – mostly highly motivated – individuals,

---

[40] Some of the interviewees thought that the instinct and pragmatism of Mr Rop played too strong a role, causing a ceaselessly shifting position on pension reform issues.

[41] The two representatives of national minorities almost always side with the ruling coalition, thus giving the majority 51 votes out of a total of 90.

with a clear division of ministries and responsibilities among the coalition partners. Quite understandably, the leading party of the coalition, the LDS, undertook pension reform as its own project, and Mr Rop (also vice president of the LDS from January 1998) was responsible for carrying it through to successful conclusion. It must be reiterated that pension reform was never seriously discussed at cabinet meetings, where it was assumed that Mr Rop would resolve issues in the appropriate forums – i.e. in meetings of the working group.

The other two members of the coalition had a completely subordinate role in the pension reform process. The SLS and Desus never came out with comprehensive pension reform proposals. Their representatives were included in the working group rather late in the process, in September 1997. Both parties had a short list of demands, which were very much targeted to their electoral base. Thus, Desus insisted on wage indexation, the introduction of a **widows' pension,** the retention of the so-called recreational supplement for pensioners, and a legal obligation for the government to finance the pension deficit. The late inclusion of the coalition partners in the preparation of the *White paper* meant that only some of their demands were addressed in that document. Nevertheless, their demands were mostly included in the 1999 PDIA, albeit some in a diluted form (such as the widows' pension).

The SLS pushed for a national pension, which is a very particular form of means-tested benefit. Of course, the pension and disability acts always contained rules for entitlement and benefit levels for various social assistance measures, but these benefits were predicated on the income (or disability) status of the recipient. With the national pension, there is no such linkage – it is a social assistance measure, but of a special type. Namely, it is means-tested, but at the personal (individual) level and not at the level of the family or household. Also, this means testing, which is unique in the Slovenian practice of social assistance, is performed just once, that is upon granting the pension, whereas most other social assistance disbursements are subject to annual renewals. Social security experts unanimously opposed its inclusion in the *White paper* and later in the PDIA. Nevertheless, Mr Rop estimated that the inclusion of a national pension in the PDIA was a very small price to pay for the support of the SLS in passing the law.

The Ministry of Finance
The Ministry of Finance played a relatively modest role in the pension reform process. This was due not only to exogenous factors, such as the fact that the

Minister of Labour, Family and Social Affairs was in charge of the pension reform team. Much can be attributed to a deliberate attitude of the Ministry of Finance, something of a 'hands-off' approach. Ministry officials were rarely present at meetings of the pension reform group. The limited role of the Ministry of Finance is reflected in the fact that, among 26 contributors to the *White paper*, there is but one official from the Ministry. Mr Gaspari stated that 'the Ministry simply did not have a team for tackling the pension reform' (interview, Gaspari). While this is certainly true, this could hardly qualify as a valid excuse for assuming a passive role.

The Minister of Finance, Mitja Gaspari, never quite warmed up to the idea of a mandatory fully-funded second pillar. Considering the fact that he served a short spell in the World Bank (September 1991–June 1992) this might appear a bit surprising. A cautious and highly respected financial expert, he considered his main task as preserving the stable fiscal position of Slovenia. He was quite concerned that the introduction of a mandatory funded second pillar might worsen the country's fiscal position in the short and medium term. Also, there were two other large government commitments 'knocking on the door', which loomed large in his mind. First, the commitment stemming from the privatization gap had to be honoured through the sale of state assets. The gap was estimated at just under USD 1 billion, or some 5.5 percent of GDP (World Bank, 1999, p. 92). Second, there were government obligations toward denationalization claimants who did not receive their nationalized assets back in kind, but were (or will be) given indemnity bonds. It is estimated that the total value of these claims will not be greater than DEM 2.4 billion (Compensation Fund, 2001, p. 2), which represents some 6 percent of GDP.[42] The commitment stemming from the privatization gap will not have direct consequences on the fiscal position of Slovenia, although the sale of assets will decrease the state's stock of capital. The claims on nationalized assets will have fiscal consequences, but not immediately – the indemnity bonds will become tradeable by 2005, and interest payments will have to be made from 2007.

On the surface, these commitments would not merit great concern by the Minister of Finance. Given the understandable but perhaps excessive concern for

---

[42] The actual value of liabilities very much depends on how much of the nationalized property will be returned in kind.

impending liabilities, Mr Gaspari was not engaged in the search for the key element required to introduce a mandatory second pillar – a source of revenue for financing the transition. That was Mr Rop's problem.

The Institute for Pension and Disability Insurance

The IPDI could hardly be regarded as a monolithic institution with a distinct view or opinion. In spite of its formal autonomy, this institution is in many ways subordinate to the MoLFSA. Thus, it is not surprising that experts from the IPDI were (and still are) extremely reticent to make any pronouncements on pension issues that have a political undertone. In other words, a public pronouncement in favour or against the mandatory second pillar would represent a breach of this bureaucracy's etiquette. Though one member of the IPDI was in the core group from the very start of the pension reform process, and several members contributed to the *White paper* and in drafting the PDIA, the IPDI could be described as neither a real proposal actor, nor a real veto actor.

Parliamentary opposition

The parliamentary opposition was fragmented and very heterogeneous, although one party did exert a tangible influence on the pension reform process. This was the ZLSD (United League of Social Democrats), which represents the reformed ex-communists. It seems that their influence was particularly strong in the FTUS, as they pressured them to accept various compromise solutions regarding the first pillar. Some of these solutions originated with the ZLSD, but were publicly proposed by the FTUS. The ZLSD was in close contact with the German and Austrian Social Democrats as well as the British Labour Party. The 'German connection', in particular, contributed to their staunch opposition to the mandatory second pillar, as the German Social Democrats have repeatedly warned that a mandatory second pillar would gradually lead to an erosion of the first pillar.

The final draft of the PDIA was very much to the liking of the ZLSD – so much so that they jokingly suggested to Mr Rop that he scrap some of the 'unreasonable' demands of the coalition partners in exchange for ZLSD parliamentary support in passing the law (interview, Pavlica).

Trade unions

In terms of popular support, the FTUS was by far the dominant trade union organization, as seen in Table 10. The FTUS is actually the reformed ex-socialist trade union, and maintains very close ties with the United League of Social Democrats (ZLSD). The FTUS was also in close contact and consultation with Bavarian trade unions, which had been spreading a second pillar gospel similar to that of Germany's Social Democrats.

Slovenian trade unions did not oppose pension reform *per se*, but opposed concrete solutions which they deemed unfair to their constituencies. Specifically, the trade unions were extremely sensitive to pensioning criteria from the point of view of blue-collar workers. They opposed a mandatory second pillar, and were in favour of a diluted parametric reform of the first pillar. Their initial opposition to the *White paper* was fierce and uncompromising. In fact, they could be described as the main veto actor as well as the main proposal actor. The large protest meeting in March 1998 was a vivid demonstration of their strength and broad support.[43] It also sent a very clear message to the government – the very real threat of a general strike.

The trade unions were particularly opposed to three points set out in the *White paper*: (1) the high retirement age of 65; (2) gender equalization of eligibility conditions and benefits; and (3) the mandatory, fully-funded second pillar. It is interesting to observe that the 'first pillar agenda' of Slovenian trade unions was somewhat similar to the one set by the Polish trade unions (Solidarity), during the pension reform in that country. Solidarity opposed gender equalization and also extracted more favourable conditions for blue-collar workers (Orenstein, 2000, p. 53, 56). However, unlike Solidarity, which supported the mandatory second pillar (Müller, 1999, p. 105), the Slovenian trade unions were strongly opposed.

The demands of the trade unions were the subject of protracted negotiations, and compromises were eventually reached. The full pensionable age was finally set at 63 for men and 61 for women. For this, credit has to be given to the ZLSD, which originally proposed this compromise. A mandatory, fully-funded second pillar was abandoned at an early stage, even before the draft law was written. The trade unions scored on a number of other important points: certain categories of workers are exempt from penalties ('maluses') for retirement before the full pensionable age, the number of years counted in the pension base was reduced from the original proposal in the *White paper* of the best 25 years to the best 18

---

[43] These were the largest demonstrations held so far in the independent Slovenia.

years, and so on. Again, credit for some of these points ought to be given to the ZLSD, for whom the FTUS seemed a convenient conduit.

The trade unions strongly rejected the mandatory second pillar, but at the same time firmly supported the voluntary second pillar and demanded that these schemes be given the most favourable tax treatment. This 'extreme disapproval – extreme approval' position may not seen quite consistent on the surface, as schemes which start as voluntary might soon result in a very large coverage of the active population and, because of favourable tax treatment, might eventually erode the tax base for social security contributions in the first pillar. However, the trade unions were not concerned about this issue. Their opposition to the mandatory second pillar was most likely caused by a never openly voiced concern that its introduction would very soon worsen the financial position of the first pillar through directly depriving its revenues. Their strong supportive position on the voluntary second pillar was quickly seized on by Mr Rop – who, after the fall of the proposed mandatory second pillar, opted for this 'second-best' solution, sugar-coated with large tax incentives.

4.2. External actors

The Phare team

An extremely important actor in the pension reform process was the Phare team. Of course, the team could not be a veto or proposal actor, but it did influence the agenda by drawing attention to the essential points that needed to be clarified or resolved. The team's cautious and circumspect posture to the mandatory second pillar seems to be in line with the general approach of Phare technical assistance teams (see Nelson, 1998, p. 14). Giovanni Tamburi, a prominent member of the team, carefully dissected the original proposals on the mandatory second pillar and exposed their most glaring weaknesses. In this sense, the Phare team strongly endeavoured to put more realism into the pension reform debate.

The World Bank

The World Bank had a strong interest in the pension reform process and was quite intent on supporting the design and implementation of the multi-pillar pension system. The first Country Assistance Strategy, approved by the World Bank and the government of Slovenia in June 1997, singled out three areas of particular mutual interest – pension reform, health reform and housing – with a total lending commitment of some USD 100 million for the fiscal period 1998–2000 to be 'flexibly' allotted among the three areas. Regarding pension reform, the Bank's activities were to be concentrated on: (1) providing advice on the design of the legal and regulatory framework for the multi-pillar pension system; (2) providing technical support on macro modelling; (3) providing support for the public awareness programme; and (4) providing technical assistance in designing a strategy for financing the transition. These activities would serve as preparatory 'groundwork' prior to loan disbursement, and they were to be financed through various grants – a Japanese grant, TACIS and the British Know-How Fund. Thus, the initial role envisaged for the World Bank in the pension reform process was in providing support for various specific tasks. It was never given the role of a major actor.

Concrete activities of the Bank included support in installing two models for pension reform simulations, as well as training staff at the Institute for Macroeconomic Analysis in their use. The grant co-financed the October 1997 International Conference on Pension Reform Issues, the workshop on Second Pillar Issues in March 1998, and a study mission of MPs and experts to Switzerland and the Netherlands in March 1998. Following the workshop, the idea of a mandatory second pillar was scrapped and the Bank's activities in this area came to a halt.[44] Not even the entire amount of the grant was disbursed, as some points in the country assistance strategy were not even touched upon – such as support for the public awareness campaign and assistance in designing a strategy to finance the transition.

The answers to the 'what' and 'why' questions regarding this rupture in cooperation between the World Bank and Slovenia in the area of pension reform are best revealed by section of the second Country Assistance Strategy, issued in April 2000:

> The Bank and Government agreed to drop plans for a Bank loan that would have helped implement pension system reform when the reform effort ran into strong political opposition that the coalition government could not quickly overcome. It was only in December 1999 that Parliament adopted a new Pension and Disability Insurance Law, which removes projected deficits in the PAYG system in the next 15 years or so, and introduces a third pillar – a voluntary fully funded system.[45] The

---

[44] It must be stressed that this setback did not impede or influence lending for other activities. In the end, lending for the housing sector (real estate registration modernization) and health sector reform totalled some USD 25 million.

[45] As is well known, the World Bank terminology reserves the term 'second pillar' for a mandatory fully-funded pillar. In the European context, the 'second pillar' denotes supplementary pension schemes, with mostly collective coverage and with certain legal obligations imposed on the employer (EU 1994: 2).

second pillar – a mandatory defined contribution pillar – currently lacks broad political support, as the fiscal strain would be significant. Nevertheless, progress in the creation of occupational funds by many large employers also on a voluntary basis could eventually lay the groundwork for a broader defined contribution pillar. While the pension reform falls short of the Bank team's recommendation and the preferences of many in Government, it reflects the outcome of a politically charged process, and provides some breathing room for future Governments to build consensus for further reforms (World Bank, 2000, p. 7).

The role of the World Bank and the International Monetary Fund should not be viewed only as fervent propagators of new approaches or preachers of new gospels. These organizations also serve as 'catalysts' for intellectual debate. Thus, the somewhat simplistic *Averting the Old Age Crisis* provoked an extremely lively intellectual debate around the world, and a particularly strong response from the International Social Security Association.[46] Following this important breakthrough in the debate on pension systems and their reform, a much greater diversification of views occurred even within the World Bank and the IMF. For example, very strong criticism of the mandatory second pillar 'mantra' was voiced by Chand and Jaeger (1996) and by Peter Heller (1998).[47] It seems that the paper by Mr Heller, known in Slovenia as the head of the IMF/World Bank team in 1995, influenced Mr Bole in shaping the case against the mandatory second pillar in Slovenia.

4.3. The actors and the reform stages

Following Orenstein (2000), the pension reform process can be divided into several phases. The first phase, *commitment building*, commenced in Slovenia with the appointment of Mr Rop as Minister of Labour, Family and Social Affairs in February 1996, and was completed with the publication of the *White paper* in November 1997. The dominant feature of this phase was that the number of actors involved in the pension reform process increased progressively, but in discrete steps. Thus, in the period from February to July 1996, when the policy document *Starting points for the reform of the pension and disability system of Slovenia* was

---

[46] A whole issue of the *International Social Security Review* (no. 3–4/95) is devoted to an argumentative rebuttal of the claims made by *Averting the Old Age Crisis*.

[47] More recently, also by Orszag and Stiglitz (2001).

submitted to the government, only a very small number of persons were involved. This core group, which included experts from the MoLFSA, the IPDI and IMAD was heavily involved in the preparation of the *White paper*. In addition to this core group, other experts were also included, but mostly for narrow and specific tasks – they were not involved in the 'big picture'. These were experts on social security law, financial markets, tax issues, and so on. After the first draft of the *White paper* (draft version 0) was completed in July 1997, members of the other two parties of the ruling coalition were included in the process. This gradual expansion did not occur by accident, but was a recognition of the veto and proposal role of these two coalition parties. They were taken on board 'just in time', and their role as potential future veto and proposal actors was thus largely neutralized. The ruling coalition thus stood solidly behind the *White paper*.

The second phase, that of *coalition building*, started in January 1998, when the negotiating working group for pension reform was formed. This was a tripartite group, composed of members from the MoLFSA, trade unions and employer associations. The employer associations were, in principle, veto and proposal actors, but their actual role in the pension reform process was marginal. They fully backed the *White paper*, and welcomed the proposal for a mandatory fully-funded second pillar. Though they were also sympathetic to some proposals expounded by the trade unions, such as a lower pensionable age than the one proposed in the *White paper* and other measures to soften the blow of the stricter pensioning rules for elderly workers, they remained loyal supporters of the MoLFSA position. Doubtlessly the strongest veto and proposal actors in this stage were the trade unions. All of their proposals were very seriously considered, and were subject to protracted negotiations. Negotiations started within the negotiating working group in January 1998, and were finally completed with the signing of the agreement among the social partners in April 1999. Would their early inclusion in the commitment phase have resulted in a shorter coalition-building phase? According to Orenstein (2000, p. 72), the exclusion of veto and proposal actors from the commitment-building stage might result in greater compromises at the coalition-building stage. In the case of Slovenia however, this does not necessarily mean that their inclusion in the commitment-building stage would have been beneficial for the pension reform process. Most close observers think that it could have well jeopardized the entire pension reform project, by requiring a diluted version of reform right from the start. Of course, coalition building exacted a high price, as the pension reform proposal was fundamentally changed in this process.

During the coalition-building process a new veto and proposal actor appeared – the Ministry of Finance. As we have seen, the Ministry proposed a parallel but partial agenda, namely a pension fund that was not envisaged in the *White paper*. This pension fund was intended to constitute a strong element of the second pillar. The idea was operationalized at the Ministry of Finance, and a law on the First Pension Fund passed in June 1999. The Ministry asserted its veto role in October 1999, shortly before the PDIA was to enter the final parliamentary deliberations (third reading), when senior officials of the Ministry strongly opposed the 'excessive' tax incentives for the voluntary second pillar. But in the end, the Ministry yielded and the path was cleared for the passage of the law. Due to the comfortable majority of the ruling coalition, the other parliamentary parties simply could not assume the role of veto actors, though the ZLSD did assume the role of a proposal actor.

The third, *implementation phase* reopened some matters which had appeared to be settled. We have observed that one of the fixed points of the Desus agenda was a satisfactory indexation rule, which in their interpretation meant wage indexation. A fairly precise rule was written into the law (article 150 of the 1999 PDIA), but was already modified by December 2000. The reason for the swift change was that a new government, elected in October 2000, deemed that the application of the rule would have very serious fiscal consequences, and therefore rushed a new indexation rule through parliament. Desus, still a member of the (new) ruling coalition, was outraged and, not to be defeated, has now proposed a more favourable indexation rule. Of course, all these rules are based on wage indexation – it is simply the details that differ, and that make a difference.[48] Desus also feels embittered and cheated because it consented to an article that adjusts existing pensions annually according to the pensions of new entrants – which are now lower because of the new benefit formulas.[49]

---

[48] Though the pension indexation rule was based on growth of wages since the 1983 PDIA, the actual rules have changed continuously. Thus, the 1983 PDIA introduced back payments effective from 1987. Back payments were abolished only in early 1996. Throughout the period, pension indexation was asymmetric – pensions were adjusted only if the growth of wages was positive. An important 'detail' is also the frequency of adjustments: monthly, quarterly or at other fixed points.

[49] Some close observers think that officials of Desus did not really understand the relevant article (article 151). It was somehow sneaked in the 1999 PDIA, and could be regarded as an element of obfuscation.

The pension reform (i.e. the 1999 PDIA) introduced numerous new actors – pension funds and pension management companies – which now have a strong interest in deepening the reform process by expanding supplementary pension schemes. These institutions were off to a very slow start, and it is impossible to predict their development, even though preconditions for their development are in place, such as very favourable tax incentives.

The trade union association FTUS is strongly pressing for the development of voluntary schemes. Its secretary general, Gregor Miklič, stated that 'the inclusion of the majority of the active population in supplementary pension schemes is instrumental in preserving old-age income security'. The presidency of the FTUS also demanded that the government of Slovenia earmark necessary funds for pension premiums for all public sector employees in its preparation for the annual budget (Delavska enotnost, 2001). This quite clearly demonstrates the desire of the FTUS to 'have its cake and eat it, too' – i.e. to have a quasi-mandatory second pillar system, but without any negative effects on the financing of the first pillar.

4.4. Deliberative forums

The main deliberative forums were working groups, which were as a rule chaired by the Minister of Labour, Family and Social Affairs. Most issues were resolved in these bodies, with the government and parliament being preciously little involved – not only in the details of reform, but also in its broad design. Thus, the working group for the preparation of the *White paper* was succeeded by tripartite groups, first named the negotiating working group (January–March 1998) and later the coordinating working group (July 1998–April 1999). This arrangement obviated the need for deliberations in other forums, and it seems that a similar arrangement also prevailed in Hungary (Orenstein, 2000 p. 39).

5. Conclusions

As Pierson (1996) has shown by examining actual changes in social policy in four very diverse countries (Britain, the United States, Germany and Sweden) one cannot speak of the dismantling of the welfare state, but rather an adaptation to 'a distinctly new environment'. It seems that Slovenia also fits into this pattern, since its pension reform did not represent a fundamental or radical shift in social policy. Although a mandatory funded pillar was very seriously considered during the pension reform process, the proposal was abandoned quite soon after the government unveiled its reform proposals in the *White paper on the reform of pension and disability insurance*. Strong opposition by the trade unions and an unsupportive attitude on the part of the Ministry of Finance contributed to the demise of this proposal. Also, due to the satisfactory fiscal position of Slovenia, the World Bank was not in a position to play a major role in the pension reform process. It seems that everything played against the introduction of a mandatory funded pillar.

Pension reform nevertheless did bring important changes, though the approach is gradualist. The parametric changes within the public pension system significantly tighten eligibility conditions and benefits, and also increase the redistributive role relative to the insurance role. It is still too early to predict to what extent the decrease in replacement rates within the first pillar will be compensated by supplementary pensions within the second pillar.

Although the changes in the Slovenian pension system could be described as radical, these is still no consensus even among experts on what constitutes radical reform.[50] Does radical reform necessarily entail a mandatory fully funded second pillar? And might not the introduction of voluntary supplementary pension schemes, with substantial tax incentives, eventually result in a large coverage of insured persons within the voluntary second pillar, but with the advantage of less fiscal strain and greater flexibility?

There is little doubt that the success of pension reform in Slovenia very much hinges on the successful expansion of voluntary supplementary pension schemes. This in turn depends on whether future collective negotiations on wages will also

---

[50] Experts even disagree about what constitutes 'pension reform' (see Chłoń and Marek 2000).

include employer contributions to the second pillar as part of the remuneration package. If such an agreement between employers and workers materializes, and if the coverage within the voluntary pillar increases rapidly, then the pension reform project may achieve the impossible – fiscal sustainability along with satisfactory pension provision for the elderly.

Acknowledgements

This work would not have been possible without the active participation of a number of persons. I owe my sincere thanks to all the informants for their readiness to be interviewed, as well as for their candid and forthcoming attitude. In addition, some of them provided valuable written material, documents and papers – for this, I am especially grateful to Dušan Kidrič, Helena Bešter, Velimir Bole, Miran Kalčič, Vitko Roš, Marjana Kanduti, Ivan Ribnikar, Janez Prijatelj and Irena Sodin.

Mirko Bandelj, secretary general of the government of Slovenia, granted me permission to review the minutes of cabinet meetings. Ana Nikšič Pentek and Sonja Šušteršič provided the necessary statistical data from the Institute for Pension and Disability Insurance. Andreja Vide Hladnik from the Institute for Economic Research provided valuable research assistance.

Finally, I am also indebted to Katharina Müller and Elaine Fultz for the probing questions and numerous suggestions following my first draft. These led me to explore some less charted territory and doubtlessly forced me to improve the text.

Of course, all errors of omission and commission remain my own. I truly hope that all participants in this collective enterprise will also feel that their time and effort has been put to good use, and that this story of the Slovene pension reform really describes 'what happened and why it happened'.

Appendix A: Interviews[51]

Belopavlovič, Nataša. State secretary, Ministry of Labour, Family and Social Affairs. 10 July 2001.
Bešter, Helena. Member of the board, Kapitalska družba. 27 June, 20 July and 10 October 2001.
Bole, Velimir. Economics Institute, Faculty of Law. 26 June 2001.
Brenčič, Stanislav. MP, People's Party (SLS). 12 June 2001.
Gaspari, Mitja. Minister of Finance. 19 July 2001.
Kalčič, Miran. Deputy director, Institute for Pension and Disability Insurance. 9 July and 8 October 2001.
Kanduti, Marijana. Public relations officer, Ministry of Labour, Family and Social Affairs. 25 July 2001.
Kidrič, Dušan. Counsellor to the government and head of the social division, Institute for Macroeconomic Analyses and Development. 15 June, 12 July and 11 October 2001.
Kolar, Milojka. State secretary, Ministry of Finance. 24 July 2001.
Kušar, Janko. President, Pensioners' Party (Desus). 6 June 2001.
Pavlica, Miloš. Vice president, United League of Social Democrats (ZLSD). 1 October 2001.
Prijatelj, Janez. Director, Institute for Pension and Disability Insurance. 5 July 2001.
Rop, Tone. Minister of Labour, Family and Social Affairs. 20 July 2001.
Roš, Vitko. Employers' Association. 18 June 2001.
Semolič, Dušan. President, Free Trade Unions of Slovenia (FTUS). 8 June 2001.
Sodin, Irena. State undersecretary, Ministry of Finance. 4 September 2001.
Škoberne, Anjuta. Professor, Faculty of Law. 20 June 2001.
Štrovs, Marko. Counsellor to the government, Ministry of Labour, Family and Social Affairs. 16 July 2001.
Vodopivec, Milan. World Bank and College for Entrepreneurship (Portorož). 26 June 2001.

---

[51] The 'position' of the interviewed persons refers to their position at the time of the pension reform process, in 1997–1999.

Appendix B: References

Bole, Velimir (1998). *Financing the Transition of the Public Pension System in Slovenia.* Working Paper Series, Economics Institute of the Faculty of Law, Ljubljana.

Bubnov-Škoberne, Anjuta (1998). 'Težko predvidljivi učinki'. *Delo,* 4 April, Ljubljana.

Bugarič, Bojan (1999). 'Privatizacija pokojninskih sistemov: (ne)varna strategija?' *Podjetje in delo,* 6–7.

Chand, Sheetal and Albert Jaeger (1996). *Aging Populations and Public Pension Schemes.* IMF, Ocassional paper, Washington, D. C.

Chłoń, Agnieszka and Marek Mora (2000). *Pension Reforms: What Stays Behind Them?* (mimeo).

Compensation fund (2001). *Annual report.*

Delavska enotnost (2001). 'V dodatno prostovoljno zavarovanje vkljuciti vse zaposlene', št. 4. 4 October.

European Union (1994). *Supplementary pensions in the European Union, supplement 4/94.* Brussels.

Fultz, Elaine and Markus Ruck (2000). *Pension Reform in Central and Eastern Europe: An Update on the Restructuring of National Schemes in Selected Countries.* ILO-CEET, Budapest.

Heller, Peter (1998). *Rethinking Public Pension Reform Initiatives.* IMF Working Paper, Washington, D. C.

IMF (1995). *Republic of Slovenia: New Challenges Confronting the Social Insurance System.* October, Washington, D. C.

Košak, Andrej (1996). 'Ekonomska neenakost zavarovancev', in *Ekonomski vidiki pokojninske ureditve,* Neven Borak (ed.). Zveza ekonomistov Slovenije, Ljubljana, 57–68.

Kuhelj, Jože (2000). *Zakon o pokojninskem in invalidskem zavarovanju, z uvodnimi pojasnili.* Uradni list Republike Slovenije, Ljubljana.

Miheljak, Vlado (2001). 'Mat brez rošad?' *Delo,* 13 October 2001.

Ministry of Labour, Family and Social Affairs (1996). *Starting Points for the Reform of the Pension and Disability Insurance System,* Ljubljana.

Ministry of Labour, Family and Social Affairs (1997). *White Paper on the Reform of the Pension and Disability Insurance in Slovenia,* Ljubljana.

Mouton, Pierre (1997). *Reform of the Current Pension System.* Technical note, Phare Project on Pension Reform, February.

Müller, Katharina (1999). *The Political Economy of Pension Reform in Central-Eastern Europe*. Edward Elgar, Cheltenham.

Nelson, Joan (1998). *The Politics of Pension and Health Care Delivery Reforms in Hungary and Poland*. Collegium Budapest, Discussion paper no. 52, Budapest.

Orenstein, Mitchell (2000). *How Politics and Institutions Affect Pension Reform in Three Postcommunist Countries*. World Bank Policy Research Working Paper, Washington, D. C.

Orszag, Peter and Joseph Stiglitz (2001). 'Rethinking Pension Reform: Ten Myths about Social Security Systems', in *New Ideas about Old Age Security*, Robert Holzman and Joseph Stiglitz (editors). The World Bank, Washington, D. C.

Pierson, Paul (1996). 'The New Politics of the Welfare State'. *World Politics*, 48, 143–179.

Ribnikar, Ivan (1989a). 'Ko bo lastnik podjetja sklad pokojninskega zavarovanja'. *Gospodarski vestnik*, 29 December.

Ribnikar, Ivan (1989b). 'Finance, lastnina, podjetje in podjetništvo'. *Bančni vestnik*, 7–8, 232–235.

Ribnikar, Ivan (1998). 'Pension reform in Slovenia – Introduction of the second or funded pillar'. *Slovenska ekonomska revija*, no. 5, 471–484.

Stanovnik, Tine and Stanka Kukar (1995). 'The pension system in Slovenia: Past developments and future prospects'. *International Social Security Review*, 48, 35–44.

Stanovnik, Tine (1997). 'Pokojninska reforma: črno v Beli knjigi'. *Naši razgledi*, 10 December.

Štrovs, Marko (1984). *Novi sistem pokojninskega in invalidskega zavarovanja*. Gospodarski vestnik, Ljubljana.

Tamburi, Giovanni (1996). *Introduction of New Pension Insurance Schemes*. Technical note, Phare Project on Pension Reform, December.

Tamburi, Giovanni (1997). *Defining the Coverage and the Financial Dimension of a Funded Second Pillar for Slovenia*. Technical note, Phare Project on Pension Reform, February.

Valant, Milan (1978). *Zgodovina socialnega zavarovanja v Sloveniji do l. 1945*. Ljubljana.

World Bank (1994). *Averting the Old Age Crisis*. Oxford University Press, New York.

World Bank (1997). *Memorandum of the President of the IBRD to the executive directors on a Country Assistance Strategy of the World Bank group for the Republic of Slovenia*. Washington, D. C.

World Bank (1999). *Slovenia: Economic Transformation and EU Accession.* The World Bank, 16 May, Washington, D. C.

World Bank (2000). *Memorandum of the President of the IBRD to the executive directors on a Country Assistance Strategy of the World Bank group for the Republic of Slovenia.* 11 April, Washington, D. C.

Chapter 3
The Political Economy of Pension Reform in the Czech Republic

Martin Mácha[1]

1. The legacy: old-age security before 1990

The Czech pension system originated in the Austro-Hungarian Empire. Under the inspiration of Bismarck's reforms in Germany, the first mandatory pension insurance scheme for salaried employees was adopted by Parliament in 1906 (De Deken, 1994). At that time, the mandatory insurance approach was considered to be the only viable solution for the protection of employees against old age and other social risks.

After the First World War, the newly formed Czechoslovakia faced a fragmented system of old-age security. Different pension schemes existed in Slovakia and Carpatho-Ukraine (which had belonged to the Hungarian part of the Empire until 1918), and Bohemia and Moravia (which had been part of Austria). Furthermore, the system could be described as a status-oriented pool of separate schemes for different categories of employees, the most privileged category being civil servants. In the new Republic, efforts were made to increase the quality and coverage of the system. A key social insurance act was passed in 1924, providing a unified pension scheme for manual workers. The chief components of retirement benefits were a flat rate and an earnings related element, pensions being granted from age 65 (Mácha, 1993).

All Czechoslovak pension schemes – for civil servants, miners, manual workers etc. – suffered badly during World War II. Some of the funds were confiscated by Nazi Germany, whereas others decreased in value due to economic developments

---

[1] William M. Mercer Associates and Former Director of the Research Institute of the Czech Ministry of Labour and Social Affairs

during the course of the war. In the meantime, the Czech government exiled in the UK had started to prepare new social reforms, which were strongly inspired by the Beveridgean model.

A milestone of post-war development was the adoption of the Law on National Insurance in 1948. This legislation combined the formerly fragmented schemes into one, providing the same conditions for all workers and employees, including the self-employed. Given the depletion of reserves, a pay-as-you-go (PAYG) system was adopted in place of the fully-funded model. The scheme included both pension and health insurance, and was to be administered by the National Insurance Company, a tripartite self-governing body (Mácha, 1993).

This law reflected the traditions of the Czech lands, as well as modern trends in social security, and was the outcome of post-war discussions on a reform concept that had been developed by the government in exile. Although the law was only passed in 1948, the year the communists took over, it was the insurance principle stipulated during the early 1940s that was put into operation. Soon afterwards, however, the approach to old-age security was fundamentally altered by the communist government. New legislation, influenced by the Soviet system, was passed in 1951–52. The pension system was fully transferred into the hands of the (non-tripartite) State Pension Administration (Law 102/1951), insurance contributions were abolished, and financing from taxation was introduced instead (Law 46/1952).

An act passed in 1956 significantly modified the eligibility criteria (Law 55/1956). In addition, the pension formula distinguished between three categories of employees. The first included the most risky occupations, such as miners and pilots, and enjoyed a shorter vesting period, a higher pension, and lower retirement age (differentiated by types of occupation). The second labour category included medium-risk occupations and also involved privileged conditions of eligibility and calculation of pension. All other occupations were subsumed in the third category, for which the level of pension was 50 percent of the average wage earned during the five years immediately prior to retirement. Although some insurance elements continued to be reflected in the computation of benefits, e.g. years of employment and income level, these were combined with the principles of redistribution and social solidarity. Another important measure included in this act was the lowering of the retirement age for the third labour category, this being fixed at age 60 for men and age 55 for women.

Economic problems increased during the second half of the 1950s, and the government was forced to reflect this in its wage and pension policies (Biskup,

2001). From 1960, a maximum benefit sum was fixed for each labour category, and pensionable income was subjected to an upper limit. This resulted in a further equalisation of pensions (Law 17/1959). Legislation promoted in 1964 differentiated women's retirement ages based on the number of their children (Law 101/1964). After this law was passed, the retirement age continued to be age 60 for men, but was set at ages 53 to 57 for women, according to the number of children raised.[2] Moreover, the vesting period was increased from 20 to a minimum of 25 years. In addition, the government began to subject pensions to personal income tax, using a progressive tax rate for higher pensions. Another measure aimed at decreasing the expenditure on pensions (see Table 1) was the restriction of the opportunity to draw a pension at the same time as receiving income from employment.

Table 1
Development of various pension system indicators, 1960–80

Indicator	1960	1965	1970	1975	1980
Population of pensionable age as a % of the total population	17.3*	18.7	20.0	19.3	18.8
Pension outlay as a % of national income**	7.1	9.0	8.2	7.7	9.0
Average pension as a % of average net wage	59.6	57.5	53.9	49.3	53.9
New pensions as a % of average net wage	70.3	60.2	61.2	56.5	64.2
System dependency ratio***	20.2	24.8	31.4	33.4	34.8

* 1961
** material net product in current prices,
*** pensioners as percentage of economically active population

Source: Adam (1983)

The pension rules created by Law 101/1964 remained in force for more than a decade without any significant changes. The purpose of Law 121/1975 was to decrease the tendency towards equalisation of benefits by abolishing the taxation on pensions, but there was still no indexation of pensions to maintain their real

---

[2] Age 53 for five and more children raised, age 54 for three or four children raised, age 55 for two children raised, and age 56 for one child raised; for childless women, the retirement age was 57.

value. Pensions were subjected to several ad hoc increases between 1975–88, but they still fell behind the price increases occurring during the same period (Biskup 2001). It was only in the late 1980s that a substantive reform of social security was undertaken. Law 100/1988, adopted just before the 'Velvet Revolution', introduced a differentiated indexation of pensions according to the year they were granted. The ceiling imposed on pensionable income was also lowered, leading to a strengthening of the link between earnings and benefits.

To sum up, the Czechoslovak pension system started out with a tradition shared with western European countries, but it was significantly altered during the communist period. The only player involved was the ruling party, and reformers approached the pension system as an instrument for fulfilling the political and ideological aims of the regime (Biskup, 2001). While being generous to some labour categories, the system discriminated against others. The pension system was financed through general taxation, and the level of pensions was not subjected to regular indexation. The system would not have been able to deal with future demographic developments, notably the ageing of the Czech population. The main aim of the reforms after 1989 was to deal with this legacy (Král, 2001).

2. Old-age security in transformation: 1990–2000

2.1. The public pension scheme

The economic reforms undertaken at the beginning of the 1990s were paralleled by fundamental social reforms. According to the first reform concept prepared by the Federal Ministry of Labour and Social Affairs in 1990, the aim of the transformation process was to create a social system which would: (1) correspond to the needs of the market economy; (2) stimulate individuals and social groups towards assuming greater responsibility for their own social situation and achieving social independence without relying on state benefits; and (3) comply with international conventions, and with the need to co-ordinate the legislation with European social insurance systems (Federal Ministry, 1990).

Transformation of the administration and financing of pensions

The most significant parametric changes in the administration and financing of the pension system occurred during 1990–92. Health insurance, which had been administered for 35 years by trade unions, and the pension scheme, administered by the State Pension Administration, were both taken over by a newly created administrative body: the Czech Social Security Administration. This state institution reports directly to the Ministry of Labour and Social Affairs, which has been responsible for pension and sickness benefit payments since 1992 (Law 582/1991).

Social insurance contributions from employers and employees were reintroduced by Law 589/1992 and imposed beginning in 1993. The contribution rate for old-age pension insurance was set at 27.2 percent, with 6.8 percent to be paid by employees and 20.4 percent by employers. The Czech Social Security Administration was the collection agent, but the resources formed part of the state budget. In the period 1993–95, the income from these contributions exceeded pension expenditures (see Table 2). The surplus was not invested, but was used for other purposes within the state budget.[3]

Table 2
Development of various pension and macroeconomic indicators, 1993–2000

Indicator	1993	1994	1995	1996	1997	1998	1999	2000
Contribution rate (%)	27.2	27.2	27.2	26.0	26.0	26.0	26.0	26.0
Revenues (CZK bn)	80.0	97.9	113.9	127.0	139.6	149.5	154.7	163.4
Pension expenditure (CZK bn)	73.6	84.2	105.8	125.6	145.1	161.8	173.0	182.2
Pension expenditure (in % of GDP)	7.2	7.1	7.7	8.0	8.7	9.0	9.4	9.6
Administration costs (CZK bn)	1.8	2.4	2.7	3.2	3.0	3.1	3.3	3.3
Revenues less expenditures, excluding administrative costs (CZK bn)	6.4	13.7	8.1	1.4	–5.5	–12.3	–18.3	–18.8
Deficit in % of GDP	–	–	–	–	0.3	0.7	1.0	1.0
Index of GDP growth	100.1	102.2	105.9	104.8	99.0	97.8	99.2	103.1
Unemployment rate	3.0	3.3	3.0	3.1	4.4	6.0	8.5	9.0
Balance of state budget (in % of GDP)	0.1	0.9	0.5	–0.1	–0.9	–1.6	–1.6	–2.4
Gross debt (in % of GDP)	24.3	26.0	31.7	35.9	40.7	43.0	42.7	43.0

Source: Ministry of Labour and Social Affairs (2001); RILSA (2001)

---

[3] The surplus occurred even though the state compensation allowance (temporary benefit paid to all children and pensioners in order to secure the most vulnerable groups against the impact of societal transformation) had been financed from pension revenues.

Finally in 1996, a special account was created within the state budget, in order to record the difference between revenues and pension expenditure. Surpluses were to be used only for the purpose of increasing benefits or covering a negative balance in pension insurance, as well as for expenses related to the collection of contributions. Even so, as a result of the surpluses in 1994–96, the contribution rate was decreased to the current 26 percent (6.5 percent for employees, 19.5 percent for employers), and the surplus disappeared (see Table 2).

In 1997 the pension system went into the red, although demographic factors were not the main cause (see Table 3). An important role was played by the existing statutory regulations, i.e. the decrease in pension contributions, the new law on basic pension insurance of 1996, and the economic crisis of 1998–2000. Together these factors caused a reduction in income for the scheme: the ratio of insured persons to persons of working age dropped, people were given credit toward a pension for certain periods during which they did not make contributions, and self-employed persons enjoyed a preferential contribution rate. At the same time, expenses increased due to the granting of favourable early retirement pensions, and also because of high claims for survivors' pensions. Further, the weak link between contributions and benefits was probably also a factor in rising costs.

Table 3
Development of demographic ratios and system dependency, 1993–2000

Indicator	1993	1994	1995	1996	1997	1998	1999	2000
Number of inhabitants 15–59 (in thousands)		6,526	6,571	6,609	6,647	6,674	6,698	
Number of inhabitants over 60 (in thousands)		1,859	1,857	1,857	1,857	1,864	1,873	
Number of insured persons (in thousands)	5,052	5,290	5,134	5,186	4,944	4,925	4,728	4,661
Number of pensioners (in thousands)	2,521	2,519	2,523	2,498	2,507	2,545	2,573	2,594
System dependency ratio*	49.9	47.6	49.1	48.2	50.7	51.7	54.4	55.7

*pensioners as percentage of contributors

Source: Adapted from Ministry of Labour and Social Affairs (2001).

During the period 1998–2000, the government tried twice to increase the contribution rate by 2.4 percent, i.e. from the current 26 percent to 28.4 percent. This adjustment, however, was not supported by Parliament.

Changes in eligibility criteria and benefits

Eligibility criteria and benefit formulas have undergone successive changes since the early 1990s. First of all, preferential treatment was removed from the pension system. The three labour categories were unified, and personal pensions were abolished (Laws 110/1990 and 235/1992).[4] Another important step taken, was that the self-employed were also included in the basic pension system (Law 110/1990).

A key parametric reform was prepared during 1993–95, and a new basic pension insurance act was passed by Parliament in 1995 (Law 155/1995). This reform, effective from 1996, retained some of the earlier elements such as a unified system for all economically active persons, the vesting period of 25 years, and the differentiation in retirement age for women according to the number of children raised. In addition, many new principles and elements were introduced. Most notably, the reform established a two-tier structure for benefits. All pensions now consist of a basic, flat rate sum and an earnings-related element. The basic amount is fixed (currently at CZK 1,310), and the government can increase this sum only by following strict rules. The basic element is paid only once, even if the beneficiary draws two or more pensions. For the earnings-related part, the average wage earned during the 10 years prior retirement is considered. This period is currently being extended by one year for each year the law remains in effect. It stands at 15 years at present, and this will be increased further until it reaches 30 calendar years by 2016.

---

[4] Personal pensions were privileges granted by the former regime to some Communist Party officials.

Table 4
Old-age pension replacement rate for different wage levels

% of average wage	Gross wage Monthly in CZK	Old-age pension Monthly in CZK	Replacement rate In %
50	6,329	5,098	80.5
70	8,861	5,554	62.7
100	12,658	6,239	49.3
150	18,987	6,802	35.8
200	25,316	7,182	28.4

Source: Ministry of Labour and Social Affairs (2001)

All earnings within the given period are incorporated into the calculation of a personal assessment base, indexed to the average wage. However, the personal assessment base is only fully incorporated into the calculation of pension up to the sum of CZK 6,600. From CZK 6,600 to 15,300 the proportion counted is 30 percent, and this falls to 10 percent for amounts above CZK 15,300.[5] This is the calculation base for the earnings-related percentage, which also takes into account the number of years insurance was paid. For old-age pensions and full invalidity pensions, 1.5 percent of the calculation base is granted for each year of insurance, the ratio being 0.75 percent for partial invalidity pensions. 50 percent of the percentage amount of a deceased person's pension is incorporated in the case of a widow's or widower's pension, while it is 40 percent for an orphan's pension. There is no ceiling on benefits, but a minimum amount has been fixed for the earnings-related element in old-age pension benefits (currently CZK 770).

The new formula was more advantageous for beneficiaries than the old one, but the flat-rate component, the reduction mechanism within the calculation base for the earnings-related element, and the ad hoc indexation mechanism resulted in a further equalisation of pensions during the period 1996–2000. Table 4 documents the very high level of equalisation and redistribution within the pension system.

Among the most important changes introduced by the 1995 act was a gradual increase in retirement age, from age 60 for men and ages 53 to 57 for women in

---

[5] These nominal thresholds are valid for the year 2001.

1995, to age 62 for men and ages 57 to 61 for women in 2007. As compensation for the increase in the retirement age, a measure fiercely opposed by various groups, very generous conditions for early retirement were introduced.[6] However, the temporarily-reduced early retirement pension was still so high that it produced a pension exceeding the regular one by 10 percent (Král, 2001). The number of early retirement pensions has grown significantly during the period 1997–2000, both because of the generosity of this benefit and the situation on the labour market in 1998–2000, when the dramatic rise of the unemployment rate forced

Table 5
Development of old-age pension levels, 1989–2000

Year	Real value of average pension		Pension/wage ratio (in %)	
	1989=100%	1993=100%	Gross	Net
1989	100.0		50.4	63.8
1990	98.4		51.6	65.2
1991	81.6		55.3	70.4
1992	79.8		52.0	67.7
1993	75.6	100.0	47.0	60.1
1994	76.3	100.9	44.4	57.2
1995	80.9	106.9	43.8	56.6
1996	87.0	115.1	43.5	56.0
1997	91.0	120.3	45.3	58.3
1998	88.9	117.6	45.9	59.0
1999	92.4	122.1	45.2	58.1
2000	92.1	121.7	44.3	57.2

Source: Ministry of Labour and Social Affairs (2001)

---

[6] The law stipulates two possibilities for early retirement. One is available two years prior to retirement age, with the requirement that the insured has accumulated 25 insurance years and has been registered for at least 180 days as a job applicant. The benefit is reduced by 1.3 percent of the calculation base for each 90 day period prior to retirement age that the pension is taken out. Upon reaching the statutory retirement age, a full pension is granted. The second possibility is to claim an old-age pension three years before reaching the statutory retirement age when at least 25 insurance years have been accumulated. In this case, the benefit reduction is lower but permanent, representing 0.9 percent of the calculation basis for every 90 days.

people to retire early. Under pressure due to the financial imbalance of the scheme, the government reacted by introducing stricter conditions for early retirement in 2001. Even though the reduction rates[7] increased in 2001 from 1 to 1.3 percent for a temporarily decreased pension and from 0.6 to 0.9 percent for a permanently decreased pension, they are still below actuarially fair rates.

The 1995 law also introduced a set of clear rules for benefit adjustment. When the overall retail price index rises by more than 5 percent, the government must increase pensions by a minimum of 70 percent of the price increase.[8] In addition, wages trends are considered in any decision on pension increases. During the period 1990–2000, pensions were increased on 15 occasions. Although the 1995 act increased the real value of pensions and the pension/wage ratio, the benefits are still well below 1989 levels (see Table 5).

2.2. The supplementary private pension scheme

Since 1994, there has been a second tier providing voluntary old-age insurance in the Czech Republic. This was introduced by Act 42/1994 Coll. and involves employees taking out supplementary insurance by joining independent, open pension funds. The system is of the defined contribution type and is administered by private, profit-making institutions (pension funds), operating in a competitive environment. There are certain social elements in the scheme, however, most notably a state contribution aimed at motivating Czech citizens to participate: each participant is entitled to a state subsidy that ranges from CZK 50 to CZK 150 per month, depending on the size of the contribution paid. Distribution of the profits of a pension fund, the vesting period, and the minimum retirement age are strictly regulated.[9]

The supplementary scheme provides a lump-sum payment or a pension, i.e. a regular payment for a fixed or indeterminate period of time (calculated according to the accumulated assets and tables of actuarial life expectancy at retirement

---

[7] These are percentage reductions in the computation base for each period of 90 calendar days prior to statutory retirement age.

[8] In 1997/98, when a severe financial crisis hit, the threshold was temporarily increased to 10 percent, with the aim of limiting pension expenditure.

[9] A maximum of only 10 percent of profits can be distributed among shareholders, 5 percent is set aside for a reserve fund, and at least 85 percent must benefit the insured persons. From 1995 to 1999 the vesting period was two years, whilst in 2000 it was increased to five years. Retirement age was 55 from 1995 to 1999, and in 2001 it was increased to age 60.

age). A termination settlement is possible if the relevant entitlement conditions are met. The following types of pension can be provided: (1) old-age pension, conditional on attainment of the age stipulated in the pension plan; (2) disability pension, conditional on retirement due to disability; (3) early retirement pension, upon expiry of a time period specified in the pension plan; (4) inheritance pension, conditional on the death of the beneficiary.[10]

A pension fund, which is a stock holding company with a special licence from the Ministry of Finance, must manage its assets carefully with the aim of securing dependable revenues. There is a special department within the Ministry of Finance supervising the operation of pension funds. Investment restrictions commit pension funds to a rather conservative portfolio (see Chart 1). Table 6 shows that the return credited to individual accounts has varied considerably over time and among the various funds, in some instances even remaining below the inflation rate.

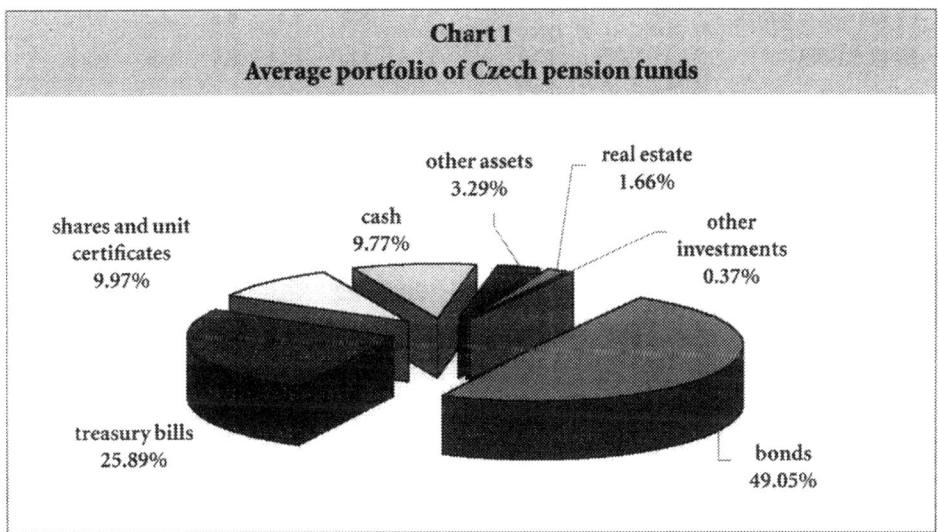

Chart 1
Average portfolio of Czech pension funds

Source: APF (2001)

During the initial years of operation, many shortcomings were detected in the scheme. The most serious were the following (Explanatory Report on the Amendments to Law 42/1994, 1999): the operating expenses incurred by the

---

[10] In the case of early retirement pensions, the insurance period must amount to a minimum of 180 calendar months, whereas the minimum is 60 calendar months in the case of disability pensions. These insurance periods may not be shortened by the pension plan.

Table 6
Development of nominal investment returns, 1995–2000

Pension fund	1995	1996	1997	1998	1999	2000
ABN AMRO PF	n.a.	n.a.	n.a.	n.a.	n.a.	n.a.
Allianz PF (dříve Allianz-Živnobanka PF)	n.a.	n.a.	8.9	9.1	6.0	3.8
Báňský a hutní PF	n.a.	n.a.	7.0	n.a.	n.a.	n.a.
Českomoravský PF	10.4	10.9	10.3	10.0	6.1	n.a.
ČSOB PF (dříve Spokoj. Českých prístavů)	0.0	16.4	8.0	10.9	7.7	5.6
Generali-Creditanstalt PF	10.3	10.6	14.6	11.4	5.3	3.6
Hornický PF Ostrava	0.0	3.5	7.8	7.7	4.4	2.0
ING penzijní fond	12.8	12.1	11.0	n.a.	6.0	4.4
PF České pojišťovny	10.3	9.2	9.6	9.7	6.6	4.5
PF Komerční banky	9.4	8.4	9.1	9.5	7.2	4.9
PF KORUNA	12.4	11.0	10.1	8.9	n.a.	n.a.
PF Všeobecné zdravotní pojišť'.	14.6	14.6	13.0	n.a.	n.a.	n.a.
Spořitelní PF	n.a.	n.a.	n.a.	n.a.	n.a.	4.2
Stavební PF	10.0	8.0	8.5	8.5	5.5	n.a.
Vojenský otevrený PF	9.5	10.0	10.0	9.7	6.7	4.1
Všeobecný vzájemný PF (Commercial Union PF)	10.1	10.2	10.0	9.3	5.0	2.9
WINTERTHUR PF	12.8	11.5	11.2	10.1	6.5	4.1
Zemský PF	11.8	7.0	7.0	7.0	7.0	5.0
Memo item: Annual inflation rate	9.1	8.8	8.5	10.7	2.1	3.9

Source: APF (2001)

pension funds were high, and not separated from the assets (see Table 7); the level of the state contribution was not adjusted to reflect changes in wages and prices, and as a result, the interest of citizens in the scheme dropped off; the participants' average contribution was rather low, and so the income of pension funds stagnated (see Table 7); the scheme was used as a short-term savings scheme by older persons instead of a long-term savings scheme for younger age groups as originally planned; and the powers of the supervision authority turned out to be inadequate.

For these reasons, an amendment to the Act on Supplementary Pension Insurance with a State Contribution was produced by the Ministry of Labour and Social Affairs. This was approved by the Czech Parliament in 1999 and has been in effect since 1 January 2000. The amendment increased the authority of state supervision of pension funds and obliged pension funds to raise their minimum capital from CZK 20 million to CZK 50 million. The main reason for these changes was to prevent the 'tunnelling' and bankruptcy of pension funds.[11] In order to discourage use of the scheme for short-term investment, the minimum savings period has been increased to five years, and savings can only be withdrawn after participants reach pensionable age or the age of 60.

Furthermore, the amendment introduced tax advantages for both employers and employees beginning 1 January 2000. An employee's annual contribution of between CZK 6,000 and CZK 12,000 is tax deductible. For a monthly contribution of up to CZK 500, a state contribution is paid; the amount above a monthly contribution of CZK 500 is tax deductible, but there is no tax concession for contributions exceeding CZK 1,500 per month. Employers' contributions to schemes taken out by their employees are tax deductible up to three percent of the gross wage. However, no state subsidy is paid towards the employer's part of the overall contribution. The employer's contributions are not regarded as taxable income for employees up to five percent of their gross wage. Employers who pay contributions will be able to offset these against social security and health insurance payments without any limitations.

Since 1994, there have been two bankruptcies and several mergers of pension funds, cutting the number of funds by more than half. At present, 18 pension funds are in operation on the Czech market, and approximately 2.4 million Czechs had joined the scheme by autumn 2001. In 2000, the clients' average monthly contribution amounted to CZK 351, while the average monthly state contribution was CZK 97. The total assets of the funds were CZK 43.2 billion, which is less than 3 percent of the GDP (see Table 7). Since the introduction of tax incentives in January 2000, a significant number of new contributors have joined the system: nearly half a million new clients have taken advantage of this opportunity. The Ministry of Labour and Social Affairs is preparing a second

---

[11] 'Tunnelling' is a special term which originated during privatisation, when revenues and property were transferred from one company to another, leaving the original company to go bankrupt.

amendment to the law to be introduced in the near future, primarily aimed at separating assets from operating costs (Concept of Pension Reform, 2001).

Table 7
Development of supplementary pension insurance, 1994–2000

Indicator	1994	1995	1996	1997	1998	1999	2000
Number of participants (in thousands)	183	1,290	1,546	1,637	1,740	2,006	2,281
Number of participants (as % of economically active population)	3.7	25.7	30.7	33.1	35.7	42.7	49.7
Total assets (in CZK bn)	0.1	4.4	11.5	19.6	28.4	37.7	43.2
Total assets (as % of GDP)	0.0	0.3	0.7	1.2	1.6	2.1	2.3
Operating costs (as % of total assets)			9.0	3.3	4.2	3.9	2.5	2.5
Average monthly contribution (amount of state contribution)	118 (43)	262 (93)	305 (103)	333 (97)	329 (93)	339 (96)	351 (97)
Average monthly contribution (as % of average wage)	1.7	3.2	3.2	3.1	2.8	2.7	2.6
Number of pension funds			44	44	38	29	22	19

Source: Adapted from Ministry of Labour and Social Affairs (2001)

2.3. Latest developments and reform proposals

In the late 1990s, demographic projections showed that the parametric reform introduced in 1996 would not be sufficient to cope with the ageing of the population in the Czech Republic (see Table 8). Therefore, a new pension reform concept was prepared by the Ministry of Labour and Social Affairs. This was officially presented for discussion in 2000 and approved by the Czech government in 2001 (Concept of Pension Reform, 2001). According to these plans, the old-age security system should continue to be based on two tiers, i.e. the mandatory pension insurance (PAYG financed) and the voluntary supplementary scheme (fully funded). In the mandatory public tier, the old-age pension/net wage ratio and the old-age pension/gross wage ratio should be 55–60 and 45 percent, respectively. Income from the supplementary schemes should reach 10 to 15 percent of the net pre-retirement income within a period of 10 to 15 years. The pension scheme as a whole should ensure adequate compensation for low, middle and upper-middle income groups.

Table 8
Demographic projections, 1995–2030

	1995	2000	2010	2020	2030
Number of inhabitants (in thousands)	10,320	10,268	10,244	10,098	9,691
Age distribution (%)					
Men:	100.0	100.0	100.0	100.0	100.0
0–19	28.0	24.1	20.3	19.3	18.2
20–54	52.4	54.5	52.0	49.4	45.6
55–64	9.2	10.5	14.4	12.6	15.1
65+	10.4	10.9	13.3	18.7	21.2
Women:	100.0	100.0	100.0	100.0	100.0
0–19	25.2	21.7	18.3	17.4	16.4
20–54	48.8	50.6	47.9	45.7	42.0
55–64	9.9	11.1	14.9	12.5	14.8
65+	16.0	16.6	18.9	24.4	26.9

Source: Ministry of Labour and Social Affairs (2001).

The following principles for pension reform are stipulated:

1. The PAYG financing of the mandatory public scheme should remain unchanged. The existing contribution rate of 26 percent, however, is not expected to be sufficient for financial balance.
2. The scheme should remain uniform, with no major variations for individual groups of insured persons such as self-employed or civil servants.
3. Redistribution should be gradually limited, while the insurance principle, i.e. the link between contributions paid and pension level, should be strengthened. The introduction of a so-called Notional Defined Contributions (NDC) scheme should be considered for the first tier. The fixed retirement age could then be replaced by a flexible retirement age.
4. The following measures are believed to improve the financial stability of the scheme:
   – stricter entitlement criteria,
   – state payments to the scheme for certain non-contributory periods,
   – a closer contribution-benefit link.

5. In order to strengthen the basic mandatory scheme and to improve financial transparency, scheme financing should be separated from the state budget. A new institution, the Social Insurance Company, should be established for this specific purpose.
6. The range of services offered within the voluntary pension tier should be broadened in the foreseeable future. In particular, occupational pension schemes, common in all advanced countries, should be introduced, as well as other services offered by commercial life insurance companies.

Based on the above principles, the Ministry of Labour and Social Affairs has prepared two draft laws which have been approved by the government and presented to Parliament as the first steps to pension reform. The Law on the Social Insurance Company would significantly alter the administration of the Czech old-age scheme and separate it financially from the state budget. The Social Insurance Company should take over all the administrative tasks of the current Czech Social Security Administration. It should be financed from a percentage of social insurance contributions to be stipulated by law, and it should comply with higher administrative and technological standards in order to cope with new tasks, such as running NDC plans. The Law on Supplementary Occupational Pensions would broaden opportunities in the fully-funded voluntary tier. According to the draft law, pension plans should be of the defined contribution type, but the defined benefit plans should be considered in the future.

In developing these proposals, the Czech government continued to reject the partial privatisation of old-age security, mainly due to the high transition costs resulting from such a move (Concept of Pension Reform, 2001). Chart 2 indicates the transition costs stemming from partial pension privatisation, assuming a newly-introduced fully-funded scheme alongside the current PAYG scheme. It also assumes that the new tier would be mandatory only for new entrants to the labour market, i.e. persons below the age of 20. Transition costs are expressed in terms of the additional percentage points that would need to be added to current pension contributions. The chart also depicts the current and future shortfall in the contribution rate to the PAYG system, irrespective of pension privatisation.

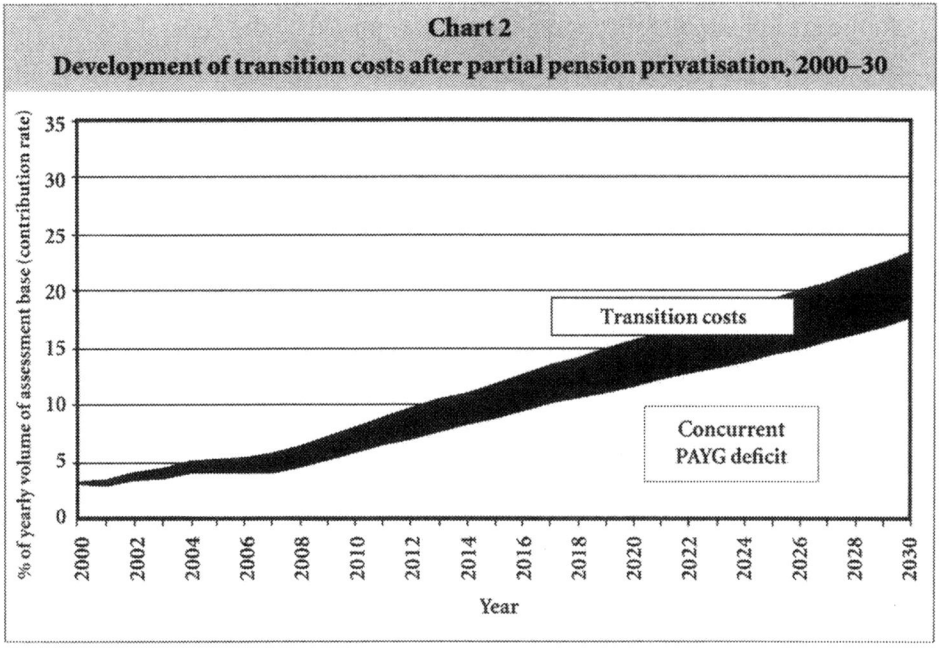

Source: Ministry of Labour and Social Affairs (2001)

Note: Estimates are based on the presumption that the contribution rate remains at the current level. Not all assumptions are spelt out in the source.

3. Explaining post-socialistic pension policy

3.1. The federal period of Czechoslovakia

After the 'Velvet Revolution' in 1989, new faces appeared on the political and professional scenes, coming primarily from academic institutions and the so-called dissent movement, as well as from the business community. 'Civic Forum', an association of these new thinkers which prepared an agenda for the first free elections in 1990, became a major political force. Among the experts engaged in designing the first principles of economic and social reform were representatives both of economic neo-liberalism and of the Prague Spring movement of 1968. At the beginning, these two groups co-operated to a reasonable extent, and their joint efforts brought about unambiguous support for the fundamental principles of market economy, civic freedom and social rights, as expressed by the 1990 election results.

In the area of social policy, a major role was played by the Federal Ministry of Labour and Social Affairs, which introduced certain new elements into the pension system, while at the same time preparing a long term strategy for social reform.[12] This first programme document, presented to the Federal Parliament in September 1990, was entitled 'Scenario of Social Reform' (Federal Ministry, 1990). This document was based on the Czechoslovak traditions of the inter-war years and the immediate aftermath of World War II. It proposed a unified obligatory pension insurance based on the principle of PAYG financing, to be administered by a self-governing public institution with tripartite bodies. Pension benefits would consist of two components: the first component was to be flat-rate and regularly indexed, the other was to be earnings-related, reflecting the specific career and wage history of the employee. The entire system was to be supplemented by additional employee insurance, to which the employer would also contribute. The contributions were to be paid into individual accounts managed by private pension funds, administered and invested under state supervision.

The first significant steps to reform were thus taken immediately after 1989, and these were widely supported across the political and civic spectrum. The abolition of the preferential pension system, the introduction of regular valorisation, and the establishment of the new administrative body, the Czech Social Security Administration, took place in 1990 and 1991. Even the abolition of labour categories, with differing benefit formulas for privileged professions such as miners and heavy industry workers, was successfully concluded after negotiations within the newly-created tripartite body.[13] In exchange, the speedy introduction of supplementary occupational pension insurance was promised by the federal government, which in any event had already been part of its new pension concept. The new pension insurance system was to be initiated by a series of reforms, approved by the federal Parliament in 1992, and known as the Social Insurance and Government Employment Policy Contributions Act.

In 1992, reform of the healthcare system was also underway, introducing principles similar to those guiding pension reform. The financing of healthcare was separated from the national budget, and mandatory health insurance

---

[12] The experts behind this were Igor Tomeš and Milan Horálek, both deputies of Petr Miller, the Federal Minister of Labour and Social Affairs.

[13] The so-called 'Council of Economic and Social Accord' consisted of representatives of the State, and of both employers and employees (trade unions).

contributions from both employers and employees were administered by a public insurance company, as well as by the occupational insurance companies which were then being created. The latter were open to all citizens regardless of their occupation. They were permitted to offer various higher-standard services within the compulsory health insurance scheme, while competing for customers.

In 1991–92, a group of pragmatic economists close to the Federal Minister of Finance, Václav Klaus, began to crystallise within the Civic Forum. Great differences of opinion emerged regarding the Forum's election manifesto, eventually leading to the disintegration of the movement which had been so successful in the 1990 elections. One of its successors was the Civic Democratic Party (ODS), created and led by Václav Klaus and advocating neo-liberal policies. Their manifesto spoke out against all contemporary and future social experiments, as well as against a corporatist or Scandinavian type of welfare state. The disintegration of the Civic Forum also led to the creation of another political party: the Civic Movement (OH). Some of its representatives were famous figures from the 'Velvet Revolution', including both Ministers of Labour – the federal one and the Czech one. These were the very people who had elaborated the fundamental principles of pension reform set out in the first programme document, 'Scenario.' The 1992 election resulted in a clear victory for the ODS, and total defeat for the OH, which did not even manage to attain the 5 percent threshold for entering Parliament.

Another key event was the decision to split the Czechoslovak federation as of 1 January 1993. The work on social reform ceased completely, with the government's attention being focused primarily on the technical and administrative division of the federation. The Minister of Labour and Social Affairs in the new Czech government led by Václav Klaus was Jindřich Vodička (ODS), and Ivan Kočárník (ODS) was appointed Minister of Finance. Minister Vodička had not taken part in the preparations for social reform in 1990 and 1991. As the former head of one of the district labour offices, he only started to become familiar with pension insurance after his appointment. As there were no experts who shared the ideas of his political party, he had to resort to consulting experts from the Ministry of Labour, most of whom had participated in the early preparations for social reform at the now abolished Federal Ministry of Labour. Several experts who did not transfer from the Federal to the Czech Ministry of Labour began to work as advisors to the Czech Social Democratic Party. These factors significantly influenced the subsequent development of pension reform.

3.2. Moving towards in-depth transformation

After the introduction of social insurance contributions in 1993, work on further elements from the federal concept of pension reform began, e.g. the key act on basic pension insurance, the separation of the pension fund from the national budget, and an act on additional employee pension insurance.

During 1993 and 1994, the relationship between the government and trade unions gradually deteriorated. The Klaus government wanted fast and effective privatisation and the introduction of market principles into many aspects of life, and considered social dialogue an unnecessary obstacle, if not a socialist anachronism. The strength of the ODS in Parliament was so prevalent that most of the government's decisions were implemented relatively easily, in spite of the lack of tripartite communication.

Achieving a balanced state budget was one of the most important priorities of that government. This explains its hesitation in separating pension finances from the national budget. In 1993–95, the income from social insurance contributions greatly exceeded expenditure on pensions, disability benefits, and unemployment benefits, which enabled the cross-subsidisation of other social benefits and services.

Furthermore, the first negative experiences with the new health insurance system began to emerge, only increasing the government's doubts about the functionality of public insurance companies within Czech social insurance, and about the efficiency of public administration in general. Healthcare expenses grew rapidly during the first years of the new system, the insurance companies' costs were high, and the collection of insurance payments was not very efficient. In contrast to this, the Czech Social Security Administration functioned well and had no problems, but autonomous management of its finances was lacking.

In these momentous years, the first signals were received from international institutions, specifically from the World Bank, concerning the need to implement radical pension reform (World Bank 1994). Given the economic situation in the country (see Table 2), the government's promotion of a strict fiscal policy and a low level of external debt, the influence of the World Bank and the International Monetary Fund (IMF) on the government was limited. Moreover, the government's declared unwillingness to copy models from abroad, or new models created by experts outside the Czech Republic, was typical of that period, although it is evident that the government did have its foreign sources of inspiration. Václav Klaus was known for his admiration of the British Prime Minister, Margaret Thatcher, and her economic and social policies. In several presentations and articles written by Klaus, there is an inclination towards the British model of state universal pensions, supplemented by various forms of supplementary schemes based on individual choice (e.g. Klaus, 1995).

Gradually, the government abandoned the concept of social reform planned in the 'Scenario' document. After ignoring proposals by Ministry of Labour experts to create a separate pension fund, the government also failed to approve the Act on Supplementary Occupational Pension Insurance, which was still based on the federal concept. It was argued that voluntary supplementary pension insurance, based on the civic principle and supported mainly by state contributions rather than employer contributions, was much more appropriate under the conditions of that time. Moreover, such an arrangement would provide supplementary insurance to citizens who are not employees (self-employed, housewives, students, etc.), as well as to employees whose employers were not able or willing to establish an employee-based scheme. For civil servants, the supplementary pension insurance with a state contribution would be the only opportunity to obtain supplementary pension insurance.

The government commissioned the Ministry of Labour and Social Affairs to come up with a proposal for a supplementary system which would not be based on the participation of employers. They should contribute only voluntarily, without being granted any tax relief. The new scheme would be fully based on the civic principle, i.e. be totally accessible to any citizen of the country. Citizens should not be stimulated to participate in the system by tax incentives. Instead, a form of motivation based on a state subsidy was chosen, which would grow proportionately to the insured person's contributions, but would be subject to an upper ceiling. At the same time, negative experiences with the development of financial and capital markets, involving the collapse of several private banks and the loss of savings, required that the new supplementary pension insurance act stipulate very strict conditions for pension fund investments, demanding a conservative composition for their portfolios.

The Act was approved in 1994, leading to the creation of 44 open pension funds set up by state banks, insurance companies, and other private entities. The competition for clients among the funds led to substantial advertising expenses and high commissions for insurance brokers. The conservative investment conditions resulted in low profitability for individual participants. Furthermore, public mistrust of financial institutions, flaws in the design of state contribution, and the disadvantageous position of employers in the system led to low contribution levels. Thus, the growth of assets administered by the pension funds was slow. However, pension funds gradually established a strong lobbyist group, the Pension Fund Association.

At the same time, a loose coalition of financial sector specialists, bank and capital market analysts, and neo-liberal economists reacted to new demographic projections with proposals for radical pension reform. Their contacts with international institutions, notably the World Bank, as well as with reformers from countries planning the implementation of radical pension reform, e.g. Poland and Hungary, inspired them to analyse the possibility of introducing a compulsory second tier of mandatory private pension funds (see e.g. Schneider, 1995; Kočišová, 1997; Kreidl, 1997). None of these analyses involved consideration of the traditions and historical developments of Czech social policy, however, and their impact on policy-making remained limited.

In 1995, a new draft law on the basic pension insurance scheme was finalised by the Ministry of Labour and Social Affairs, drawing heavily on the first federal concept of pension reform. Yet it is interesting to note, that the indexation rules and the pension formula itself also included elements enabling a gradual shift to a more universal model of state pensions. It was only in this way that Minister Vodička could overcome Klaus' initial objections.

The proposed bill on the basic pension insurance scheme alarmed the trade unions, which until then had been protesting only occasionally and not very forcefully. In 1995, they organised a rally against the new draft law, which turned out to be the largest demonstration seen in Prague since 1989. Their main criticisms were directed against the raising of the retirement age and the extended delay in separating pension insurance from the state budget.

The demonstration, which took place on the Old Town Square in Prague, frightened some of the coalition partners of the ODS. One of them, the Christian Democrats (KDU-ČSL), rejected the law for not having been sufficiently discussed and for lacking societal consensus. The ODS started negotiations in Parliament and in the end, the Českomoravská unie středu (Czech and Moravian Union of the Centre), a small party, which was not a member of the government coalition, voted for the law. In exchange, more favourable conditions for early retirement were introduced, and the government committed itself to the creation of a special pension account within the state budget.

The new Law 155/1995 Coll., with effect from 1 January 1996, was not only criticised from the left of the political spectrum. It was already clear that the new benefit formula would cause a gradual increase in the costs of the pension system as a whole, while also increasing the compression of benefit levels and resulting in differences between new and old pensions. Experts in demographic development considered the increase in the retirement age to be insufficient, given that the transition period of ten years would not keep pace with the increase in life expectancy in the Czech Republic. Nevertheless, the new pension law complied with European legislation and with the binding conventions of the Council of Europe and of the International Labour Organisation (ILO).

3.3. Approaching the economic crisis

The 1996 elections showed the increasing popularity of the Czech Social Democratic Party (ČSSD) which, together with the trade unions, expressed strong criticisms for Klaus' economic and social reforms. Although the ODS won the elections, the party could not even obtain a majority in Parliament in co-operation with its traditional coalition partners, the KDU-ČSL and the ODA. Lengthy negotiations with ČSSD, which had won the second largest number of seats in Parliament after the ODS, were not successful in establishing a minority coalition government. Finally, two ČSSD Deputies decided to support the programme of the coalition government, enabling the ODS and its coalition partners to continue with their policies.

In 1997, a fiscal crisis and the beginning of economic stagnation (see Table 2) forced the minority government to adopt a so-called 'austerity package' that affected the pension system. The rules for the valorisation of pensions were temporarily changed and the counting of certain substitute insurance periods in which no contributions were made was restricted. In the autumn of that year, the government, struggling to overcome the critical economic situation, received its final blow when inconsistencies in ODS party accounts came to light. After this scandal, the other two coalition parties – the KDU-ČSL and the ODA – resigned from the government, which subsequently tendered its resignation. The formation of a new government of 'specialists', which was to be in power until extraordinary elections were held in 1998, was entrusted to the governor of the Czech National Bank (ČNB), Josef Tošovský. In co-operation with President Havel, he chose cabinet members from among specialists, as well as from the former coalition parties and from a splinter wing of the ODS, which consequently founded a new liberal party, the Unie Svobody (Union of Freedom).

Stanislav Volák was appointed Minister of Labour and Social Affairs in the new government of specialists. He was an ODS deputy of many years' standing, specialising in social issues. At the end of 1997, he left the ODS to become a co-founder of the Union of Freedom, as did the new Minister of Finance Ivan Pilip, who was known for his close contacts with financial and banking experts who supported the neo-liberal doctrine of pension reform. Both brought to their Ministries an impetus toward radical reform for the pension system, along Polish and Hungarian lines.

Nevertheless, analyses by the Ministry of Labour and Social Affairs showed that such a reform would be risky. In addition, the trade unions, with whom the new temporary government revived constructive dialogue, were not willing to accept this variant on reform. Neither would the powerful ČSSD accept such a model for the Czech Republic. In preparation for the election campaign, this party returned to concepts originating from the time of the Czechoslovak Federation. Its expert commission was made up of specialists who had contributed significantly to the first federal concept of social reform.

At the same time, the Ministry of Labour and the Czech Administration of Social Security were concentrating on the mounting deficit in the pension account, on the decrease in the real value of pensions as a consequence of austerity measures, and on improving the manner in which insurance contributions were to be collected from companies affected by the economic crisis. Growing unemployment created additional pressure for early retirement, and the financial balance of the system began to slip into the red.

Deteriorating conditions for pensioners motivated their civic as well as political associations to take action. Their political party, the Association of Pensioners for a Secure Life (DŽJ), heavily criticised the social policies of the preceding period, including Law 155/1995, and promised to improve the position and social conditions of Czech pensioners. Voters seemed very responsive to these promises, and the support for this party peaked at 15 percent a few weeks before the elections. The Czech Social Democratic Party suffered the most from this shift of allegiance, as traditionally they were strongly supported by the elderly among the electorate.

In the period just preceding the elections, the ODS began to recover from the financial scandal, and declared its intention to continue the reforms it had begun, including pension reform. It did not specify, however, whether it would promote the three-pillar model of old-age pensions. Its support gradually reached 20 percent, to the detriment of the Union of Freedom, which had been very popular at the beginning of the year, being the only party to advocate World Bank-style pension reform in its election manifesto.

3.4. The social democratic government

The June 1998 elections resulted in a stalemate. Although the ČSSD won the elections, it lacked the four percent of votes obtained by the Association of Pensioners for a Secure Life (which ultimately did not even gain representation in Parliament) and needed in order to form a single-party social democratic government. Finding a coalition partner to implement ČSSD policies was not a simple task. The Union of Freedom refused to negotiate with the Social Democrats, while the KDU-ČSL were not willing to join a coalition with the social democrats without the participation of the Union of Freedom. In the end it was the ODS, now the second strongest party in Parliament, which pledged, under specific conditions, to abstain from voting against the ČSSD government, and by doing so made their minority government possible.

The agreement concluded between the two former political rivals not only stipulated conditions for further economic reforms, such as a quick privatisation of all state banks and companies, and the deregulation of energy and rent prices. It also stipulated that the tax burden on individuals and businesses should not be increased, and that pension reform was to be continued. This was later interpreted as implying that a concept of pension reform would be presented to Parliament before the end of 2000.

The Ministry of Labour and Social Affairs was taken over by Vladimír Špidla, who had worked for many years on the Parliamentary social committee and on specialised committees of the ČSSD. He was followed to the above Ministry by an expert from the Czech and Moravian Association of Trade Unions, Jiří Rusnok, who became Deputy Minister for social insurance. Since 1998 there have been three Ministers of Finance, the latest being Špidla's former Deputy Rusnok. In the Czech Republic, the Ministry of Finance has never interfered with the pension reform concepts of the Ministry of Labour, which at present even has its 'own man' in the Ministry of Finance.

It was in 1998 that under Špidla's administration the Ministry of Labour and Social Affairs produced a proposal to increase the contribution rates to the basic pension insurance scheme, in order to stabilise the pension system deficit. Because the opposition agreement stipulated a constant tax burden, however, this draft was not passed by Parliament. On the other hand, an amendment to the law on supplementary pension insurance with state contribution, which had been prepared by Labour Ministry experts, received parliamentary approval in 1999. Both the ČSSD and the opposition were keen to encourage more dynamism in the voluntary pension scheme. Measures were taken to increase deposit security for participants, and employers' participation in the system was encouraged and magnified by the introduction of tax incentives (see 2.2). Commercial insurance companies began to show considerable interest in the pension reform. By offering their expertise to Parliament and by negotiating with Ministries, they ensured very similar tax conditions for the participation of employers and employees for a specific life insurance product, implemented by an amendment to the tax law effective beginning 1 January 2001.

In the meantime, at the Ministry of Labour and Social Affairs, preparations for pension reform were completed by the year 2000. The discussions on pension reform had been gathering pace since the social democratic Government had come to power. In 1999, a sub-committee for pension reform was set up in the Senate. Experts from the Ministry of Labour and Social Affairs visited Poland, Hungary, Sweden, the Netherlands, Italy, Germany and other countries, in order to observe pension reforms first hand. In June 2000, a temporary commission for pension reform was established in Parliament with aims similar to the Senate sub-committee. This commission met three times during the course of the year 2000. The need to stabilise the present system forced the Government to accept a proposal from experts at the Ministry of Labour and Social Affairs to limit the advantageous conditions of early retirement (see 2.1). The government proposal was passed by Parliament without any major difficulties, and it came into effect in mid 2001.

In November 2000, the government presented a proposal to Parliament concerning the establishment of a Social Insurance Company, i.e. the transformation of the state-run Czech Administration of Social Security into a public institution able to administer individual insurance accounts, including an NDC system if necessary. In 2001, the government approved a law on employees' supplementary pension insurance, which had been prepared by the Ministry of Labour and Social Affairs based on the principles recommended by the expert group of the PHARE-Consensus programme (Callund Consulting, 1999).

A major discussion on the modernisation of the law on the basic pension insurance scheme seems to be on the horizon, including the possibility of a further rise in the retirement age, a tightening of eligibility, a change in the pension formula, to make it less redistributive, and the introduction of actuarial elements into the calculation of retirement benefits. In the course of time, a transition to an NDC plan as part of the basic system may be considered.

There has generally been broad and constructive discussion at official levels, i.e. in the Chamber of Deputies, in the Senate and at many conferences sponsored by international organisations, including the World Bank and the ILO. It has proved very difficult, however, to find political consensus on the latest reform concept prepared by the Ministry of Labour and Social Affairs (Concept of Pension Reform, 2001).

3.5. Prospects

At this point, pension reform in the Czech Republic is dependent on further developments in the political arena, with elections coming in 2002. The right-wing parties – the ODS and the Union of Freedom – call for more radical change, though their manifestos refer to somewhat different reform principles. Although the Union of Freedom agrees with the transformation of the Czech Administration of Social Security into a Social Insurance Company, it will not support this proposal without agreement on further reforms.

Recently, an alternative concept drawing on the three-pillar model has been put forward in general terms as part of the Union of Freedom programme of social reform. This party will enter the election campaign as a member of the so-called Coalition of Four, with two other small, liberally oriented parties and the KDU-ČSL. Current forecasts seem to indicate an election victory for them. However, in the sphere of social policy, the KDU-ČSL has adopted a very reserved attitude to neo-liberal concepts, so it is not clear whether a future Coalition of Four government would support radical pension reform.

High transition costs may also continue to discourage experts at the Ministry of Finance. On the other hand, should Ivan Pilip – at present Deputy Chairman of US and shadow Minister of Finance for the Coalition of Four – return to the position of Minister of Finance, several neo-liberal economists who advocate the 'new pension orthodoxy' would probably follow him to the Ministry to prepare an alternative pension reform scenario.

The ODS has maintained electoral support at the 20 percent level. Klaus is notorious for his ability to surprise, but his potential for cooperating in a coalition is rather limited. The ODS manifesto is not yet available, but statements from the ODS expert in social policy, the Deputy Chairman of the party, and a shadow Minister of Labour and Social Affairs, do not indicate that they would necessarily approve an obligatory funded second pillar. It is unclear what type of reform the ODS would support in a government with the Coalition of Four.

ČSSD electoral support has been falling during the 1998–2000 period, recently matching that for the ODS. In the election campaign, the social democrats are sure to abide by their concept of pension reform, but after the election it will be just as difficult for them to win the broad support of other political parties for that concept as it proves to be now. An agreement would most likely be possible with the KDU-ČSL, but that party is bound by the common policy of the Coalition of Four, where the proposals and views of the Union of Freedom have recently been gaining ground. The Social Democrats enjoy the support of the trade unions, which would intensify the pressure for further reform, but it does not appear that this would be sufficient to guarantee implementation of their concept.

The future of pension reform is therefore uncertain at the moment, and its direction and momentum can be clarified only after the 2002 elections.

4. Stages of reform and the role of different players in the pension reform process

Three important stages of reform can be distinguished, all of which are reflected in decision making and implementation over the past decade.

The first strategy can be characterised as 'the federal concept.' Predictably, it can be dated from 1989 to the collapse of the federation in late 1992. Its main principles are reflected in the first drafts of pension reform at the beginning of the 1990s. There was an inclination towards the PAYG pension insurance model with a strong earnings-related element, administered and financed in accordance with the classical social insurance system, i.e. establishing a public pension fund administered on a tripartite basis. With regard to the second pillar, there was an attempt to introduce a model involving voluntary occupational schemes.

The second stage began when the liberal-conservative coalition gained a parliamentary majority in the 1992 elections, and it lasted until 1997. During this period, the key reforms implemented were a compromise between the principles of the 'federal concept' and the neo-liberal model. As noted above, political statements were made and expert analyses were available proposing pension privatisation, taking into account the ageing of the Czech population, international experience, and the World Bank blueprint. However, these were vague and did not result in concrete steps to reform.

The third stage began in 1997 when left-wing parties became more influential in Parliament, but they were part of minority governments. This last phase has been characterised by broader public debate about the future of pension security, and a balance of public/political support for the 'liberal' and 'continental' reform concepts. Although pressure was put on decision-makers and political figures by the rising deficit in the pension system and new demographic projections, a formal pension reform concept was not introduced until the end of the year 2000.

It is clear from section 3 that the different stages in the reform process were dominated by differing participants and several conflicting interest groups. In the following, the key figures involved in Czech pension reform over the last ten years will be identified, in order to evaluate their relative strengths and identify them as 'main' and 'secondary' actors according to Müller (1999), and as 'proposal' or 'veto' figures according to Orenstein (2000).

Ministry of Labour and Social Affairs versus Ministry of Finance

The Ministry of Labour and Social Affairs should be identified as the principal actor. During the entire period examined, the Ministry of Labour took the lead and was the strongest proposal figure – in fact, the only one. It did not challenge the advantages of the mandatory second pillar, but pointed out the related risks, emphasising that fundamental parametric reform would be sufficient to make Czech old-age security sustainable in the future. The Ministry of Labour and the Ministry of Finance never opposed each other openly, and apart from some minor cases (e.g. Ivan Pilip's political statements supporting the new pension orthodoxy), they mainly acted in line with each other. More precisely, experts from the Finance Ministry were in line with the key player – the Ministry of Labour. Interestingly, the Ministry of Finance did not change its passive role even after pension insurance went into the red and the fiscal deficit began to increase. There are two main reasons for this: there were no social security experts among its staff, and there was no real pressure on the Ministry of Finance from the IMF and the World Bank, since the Czech Republic never had significant debts.

Trade unions

The trade unions, especially the Czech Moravian Chamber of Trade Unions (ČMKOS), can be identified as a veto figure opposing radical reform. While their experts have been sympathetic to the Ministry of Labour approach, more radical trade union leaders within ČMKOS have tended to support the policy preferences of old-age pensioners' organisations and pensioners' parties. They believe that only PAYG financing can secure the real value of benefits and keep living standards of old-age pensioners in step with economic developments in the country. They were opposed to the introduction of a mandatory savings system because of their view that old-age pensions should not be an instrument for achieving macroeconomic goals. Their most common objections to a mandatory saving system are that it is not able to protect pensions against inflation, and it tends to involve high marketing and administration costs. Their experts, who later joined the Ministry of Labour – most notably key pension reform figure Jiří Rusnok, Deputy Minister of Labour in 1998–2001 and Minister of Finance from mid-2001 – were also in favour of proposing a large-scale expansion of supplementary pension schemes on a voluntary basis. They are the closest political allies of the Czech social democrats, although in 2001 they opposed the tightening of eligibility criteria for early retirement, as legislated by the social democratic government. They could play a significant role in the process in the future, although no formal veto points are granted to them within the Czech institutional framework.

Employers

Employers and their organisations have been secondary actors in the reform process, mainly supporting pension privatisation. Their statements have not been very consistent during the past decade, and they have never had any real partner in the exploration of their ideas and principles. However, as they could become a veto figure in the future if the tripartite bodies gain more weight, they must be considered as a potentially relevant player. Employers are often considered to be a non-radical figure, with the potential to compromise.

Financial sector experts

In the Czech Republic, the move from the current PAYG system towards a funded scheme has been proposed mainly by neo-liberal economists and bankers, especially from research departments of banks and investment companies. These neo-liberal economists criticise the PAYG principle, pointing out the need to reduce high government expenditure. In their opinion, the funded system is advantageous because it limits the government's ability to interfere with the economy. It may also increase investment capital, reduce moral hazards, and strengthen personal responsibility. A similar approach has been taken by the Czech National Bank, which considers that a new system with a mandatory funded tier would bring about higher rates of domestic savings, which in turn would enable economic growth. This group of experts can be seen as the most consistent supporter of a shift from PAYG to fully-funded pension financing in the Czech Republic. They have often been visible in the pension reform arena, publishing several analyses between 1995–99 (see, e.g., Schneider, 1995; Kočišová, 1997; Kreidl, 1997). They have never converted their analytical work into an alternative proposal, however, although they could have acted as a proposal figure. Their closest political ally is the Union of Freedom, who are the favourites to win the 2002 election, and they could well serve this party as advisors in the preparation of future reforms. Should the social democrats win the next election, however, they would remain at a critical distance as secondary actors in future pension reform.

Pension funds

Supplementary pension funds, grouped together in the Pension Funds' Association, represent another relevant interest group. On the one hand, they fear that the introduction of new elements into the pension system, such as employer-sponsored occupational plans or a mandatory funded second tier, might rob them of clients if they are not entrusted with the administration of these new plans. On the other hand, they could benefit greatly from such reforms if they do end up running the new schemes. They present themselves in the mass media, offering to play a role within the framework of an appropriate future pension scheme. They are unlikely to have an important direct role as proposal or veto actors in the future, but could influence their clients and the public with their approach to pension reform.

Universities and research institutions

Another group promoting a change in pension financing are demography experts – university-based researchers – who have studied the changes that will occur in the demographic structure of the Czech Republic. They claim that the ageing of the population will be more substantial and take place more rapidly than present forecasts show. Most of them have proposed raising the retirement age and changing the current financing system into a funded scheme. Influenced by radical pension reforms in Poland and Hungary and the latest world-wide trends, they are likely to be supportive of a substantial parametric reform. Nevertheless, this group of characters is very inconsistent, and many differing opinions can be found among them. Their expertise will therefore serve the particular dominant players who find it to be in line with their own approach to pension reform.

International institutions

Over the past ten years, there has been no direct influence in the Czech pension reform arena from international organisations such as the World Bank, ILO, OECD or the European Commission. It should be emphasised that neither economic development (decisive for the World Bank), social development (decisive for the ILO) nor the state of social legislation (decisive for the European Commission) have been in such a critical state as to enable experts from these institutions to act as dominant figures in Czech pension reform. Furthermore, latest developments seem to indicate that the 'new pension orthodoxy', stimulated by the World Bank in the mid-1990s, has been replaced by a more cautious approach to pension reform in Central and Eastern Europe.[14] A recent IMF paper (Laursen, 2000), as well as the latest World Bank report (World Bank, 2001) are still quite critical of the developments in the Czech pension system. They support most of the current activities of the Ministry of Labour directed at further pension reform, but do not mention the need to establish a mandatory fully-funded second pillar. Still, they continue to recommend that a funded scheme should be considered in the Czech Republic. In view of the fact that the Czech government is not planning to take out a loan for the support of pension reform activities, it does not seem likely that these or other international institutions will be able to influence the future course of pension reform to any greater extent than they have in the past.

---

[14] For some recent criticism of the 'new pension orthodoxy' see Orszag and Stiglitz (2001).

Public opinion

The way the public perceives the urgency of pension reform is reflected by the fact that they form two groups of almost equal size – those in favour of and those opposed to reform. 46 percent of respondents find the present old-age security arrangements fully or partially acceptable for the future, while 54 percent call for substantial changes, or the creation of a totally different pension system. The majority of people are aware of the difficulties facing the old-age security system in the future. There is, for instance, high awareness of the fact that the population is getting older, and that the number of people financing pensions is decreasing (about 90 percent of respondents). 58 percent of respondents share the opinion that cutbacks will be necessary in the future, since the pension scheme is too expensive (PHARE, 1998). Yet people still expect a major part of their old-age security to be provided by the basic pension scheme, ensuring them a 60 percent replacement rate (Večerník, 2001).

Distribution of support

In order to portray a clear picture of supporters of, and opposition to, various reform concepts and approaches, a synoptic table has been produced. This table identifies the positions of different players on a positive-neutral-negative scale with regard to pension reform (see Table 9). The players considered are the following:

Expert and interest groups:
Ministry of Labour and Social Affairs – MOLSA
Ministry of Finance – MF
Financial institutions (Czech National Bank, banks, financial analysts) – FI
University and research institute experts – RE
Trade unions – TU
Employers – ER

Political parties:
Czech Social Democratic Party – ČSSD
Civic Democratic Party – ODS
Union of Freedom – US
Christian Democratic Union – KDU-ČSL
Communist Party – KSČM

Table 9 Positions of political figures on pension reform proposals

VARIOUS reform steps	Scale of support recognised among different characters			
	Strong support		Neutral stand	Strong disagreement
Parametric Reform				
Increase retirement age to 63	US ODS KDU-ČSL ČSSD FI MF MOLSA RE ER		TU	KSČM
Increase insurance contribution rate	ČSSD MOLSA RE MF		KDU-ČSL KSČM TU ER	US ODS FI
Introduction of state contributions	ČSSD KDU-ČSL US MOLSA TU RE MF		KSČM ER	US ODS FI
Shift from state to public administration	ČSSD KDU-ČSL US MOLSA MF TU RE ER FI		ODS	KSČM
Tightening eligibility criteria	US ODS FI MOLSA MF RE ER		KDU-ČSL ČSSD TU	KSČM
Substantial Parametric Reform				
Increase retirement age to 65	ODS US FI RE ER MOLSA MF		KDU-ČSL	ČSSD KSČM TU
Flat-rate pension	ODS FI		ER	US KDU-ČSL ČSSD KSČM MF MOLSA RE TU
NDC Reform				
Flexible retirement age and NDC pension plan	US ČSSD KDU-ČSL MOLSA FI MF RE		ODS KSČM ER TU	
Voluntary occupational pension scheme	ČSSD KSČM MOLSA MF TU RE ER		KDU-ČSL FI	US ODS
Structural Reform				
Introduction of mandatory fully-funded pillar	FI	US ER	KDU-ČSL ODS RE MF MOLSA	ČSSD KSČM TU

Source: Based on interviews with selected players in summer 2001 (see Appendix)

5. Conclusions: problems and policy choices

Reforms were begun in the Czech Republic when economic conditions were relatively stable, unemployment was low and social conflict was absent. The conditions were thus ideal for the implementation of an expert-led reform process. The paradox of neo-liberal discourse combined with a cautious social policy is characteristic of Czech development during the 1990s (Müller, 1999). Discussions on pension reform focused mainly on the level of security to be provided for citizens by the mandatory public pillar. The proposal figures who dominated in the 1990s supported individual responsibility for future retirement on the one hand, and a traditional model of the welfare state on the other. The voices of the 'new pension orthodoxy' were not loud enough at that time to influence this argument significantly.

The situation at the beginning of the 21st century is different. Pension system imbalances have drawn attention to the urgent need to implement fundamental pension reform in the near future. This opinion is shared by the majority of figures in the pension arena. Having observed ten years of developments in the Czech Republic and other European countries, all influential groups place a decision on the course of further pension reform high on their agendas.

The dynamic development of supplementary pension insurance and commercial life insurance since the introduction of broad tax incentives provides evidence of the great awareness people already have concerning the future of the public pension system, and their acceptance of individual responsibility for retirement income.

It is clear that the final decision on pension reform is in the hands of the politicians, although it will be influenced by other figures and pressure groups, such as the trade unions and pensioners' associations at the one end of the opinion spectrum, and the financial sector lobby at the other. These secondary actors are only likely to become influental, however, if one single political group tries to follow its own path to reform without seeking broader consensus.

A compromise resulting in extensive parametric reform therefore appears to be the most likely scenario in the near future – albeit after the next elections in mid 2002. This will probably include promotion of the NDC model, and a further push for development of the voluntary supplementary schemes.

Appendix A: Background interviews with key reform figures

The following experts and figures were interviewed in summer 2001:

Bartoš, František, senator, Christian Democratic Union – Czech Popular Party (KDU-ČSL)
Benešová, Libuše, vice-chairman of Civic Democratic Party (ODS)
Dolejš, Jiří, vice-chairman of the Communist Party of Bohemia and Moravia (KSČM)
Falbr, Richard, senator, chairman of Czech-Moravian Chamber of Trade Unions Federation (ČMKOS)
Foltýn, Ivo, chairman of the board of directors and general manager, Pension Fund 'České pojišťovny' (PF ČP)
Frankl, Michal, expert, Union of Freedom (US)
Hoideker, Jiří, director of Czech Administration of Social Security
Hrabě, Jan, expert, Ministry of Industry and Transport
Illetško, Petr, general manager and vice-chairman of the board of directors, Pension Fund 'Vojenský otevřený' (VOPF); president of the Association of Pension Funds in the Czech Republic
Král, Jiří, head of department, Ministry of Labour and Social Affairs
Křivohlávek, Václav, head of department, Ministry of Finance
Mráz, Vladimír, chairman of the board of directors and general manager, 'Kooperativa' insurance company; president of the Association of Insurance Companies in the Czech Republic
Rusnok, Jiří, Minister of Finance, Czech Social Democratic Party (ČSSD)
Semmel, Edgar, vice-chairman, Union of Pensioners of the Czech Republic
Špidla, Vladimír, first vice-premier minister and chairman, ČSSD
Štěch, Milan, senator, vice-chairman, ČMKOS; ČSSD
Šulc, Jaroslav, deputy Minister of Finance
Tůma, Zdeněk, governor; Czech National Bank (ČNB)
Volák, Stanislav, senator, US

Appendix B: References

Adam, Jan (1983): *The Old Age Pension System in Eastern Europe: A Case Study of Czechoslovak and Hungarian Experience*, Osteuropa-Wirtschaft, 28 (4), pp. 276–96
APF (2001): *Supplementary pension insurance with state contribution 1994–2001*. Association of Pension Funds of the Czech Republic.

Biskup, Jiří (2001): *Geneze právních úprav československého důchodového zabezpečení od roku 1948 do roku 1990,* Národní pojištění, (8–9), pp. 4–11.

Callund Consulting (1999): *Employers Sponsored Occupational Pensions: Feasibility and Perspective in the Czech Republic.* Final Report of the PHARE–Consensus Project, mimeo.

De Deken, Johan Jeroen (1994): Social Policy in Post-war Czechoslovakia. The Development of Old-Age Pensions and Housing Policies During the Period 1945–1989. EUI Working Paper SPS 94/13, Florence: European University Institute.

Election programmes of Czech political parties and government proposals, 1990–2001, mimeo.

Federal Ministry of Labour and Social Affairs (1990): *Scenario of Social Reform.* Prague, mimeo.

Fultz, Elaine and Ruck, Markus (2000): *Pension Reform in Central and Eastern Europe: An Update on the Restructuring of National Pension Schemes in Selected Countries.* ILO-CEET Report No. 25. Budapest: ILO-CEET.

Klaus, Václav (1995): *What is happening in pension reform?* Lidové noviny, No. 8/135, pp. 4.

Král, Jiří (2001): *Vývoj po roce 1990 a hlavní principy další reformy,* Národní pojištění, (8–9), pp. 12–20.

Král, Jiří and Martin Mácha (forthcoming): *Transformation of Old-Age Security in the Czech Republic,* forthcoming in: Winfried Schmähl and Sabine Horstmann (eds), *Transformation of Pension Systems in Central and Eastern Europe.* Cheltenham, UK and Northampton, MA, USA: Edward Elgar.

Kočišová, Jana (1997): *Analysis of international experiences for use in transformation of pension insurance.* Final Report of MPSV project. Prague: Czech Commercial Bank.

Kreidl, Vladimír (1997): *Reform of the pension system.* Prague: The Civic Institute.

Laursen, Thomas (2000): *Pension system viability and reform alternatives in the Czech Republic.* Working Paper WP/00/16. Washington: The International Monetary Fund.

Mácha, Martin and others (1993): *Suggestions for the development of the Social Insurance Scheme from the point of view of Global Trends and Foreign Experiences.* Research Institute of Labour and Social Affairs.

Mácha, Martin (1999): *Political Figures and Reform Paradigms in Czech Old Age Security,* in: Katharina Müller, Andreas Ryll and Hans-Jürgen Wagener (eds),

Transformation of Social Security: Pensions in Central-Eastern Europe. Heidelberg: Physica, pp. 247–257.

Mácha Martin and others (2000): *Human development report of the Czech Republic 1999.* VUPSV-UNDP.

Ministry of Labour and Social Affairs (2001): *Concept of Pension Reform*, Prague, mimeo.

Ministry of Labour and Social Affairs (2001): *Pension Reform: Approach MPS*, Prague, CD-ROM.

Mora, Marek (2000): *Pension Policy in the Czech Republic (lessons from a comparative study with Hungary and Poland)*, Prague Economic Papers, No. 1/2000, pp. 47–70.

Müller, Katharina (1999): *The Political Economy of Pension Reform in Central-Eastern Europe.* Cheltenham, UK and Northampton, MA, USA: Edward Elgar.

Müller, Katharina (2001): *The Implementation of Pension Privatisation in Latin America and Eastern Europe – A Cross-Regional Comparison.* Paper prepared for the joint IIASA World Bank Workshop on 'The Political Economy of Pension Reform', Laxenburg, Austria, April 5, 2001.

Orenstein, Mitchell (2000): *How Politics and Institutions Affect Pension Reform in Three Post-communist Countries.* World Bank Policy Research Working Paper 2310, Washington, DC.

Orszag, Peter R./Stiglitz, Joseph E. (2001): *Rethinking Pension Reform: Ten Myths About Social Security Systems.* In: Holzmann, Robert/Stiglitz, Joseph E. (eds): New Ideas about Old Age Security. Toward Sustainable Pension Systems in the 21st Century. Washington, DC: The World Bank, 17–62.

PHARE (1998): *Monitoring the development of social protection reform in the CEEC – I.* 1998–1999. Final Report of the PHARE – Consensus Project, Pantheion.

RILSA (2001): Bulletin No. 16. Prague, mimeo.

Schneider, Ondřej (1995): *State Pension System – a time bomb?* Prague: The Liberal Institute.

Večerník, Jiří (2001): Pension System in the Czech Republic: From Reform to Non-Reform. Forthcoming in: Kalb, Don/Kovács, János M. (eds): Comparative Institutional Reform in Social Policy. East-Central Europe in a European Context (1989–2001). Vienna: Institut für die Wissenschaften vom Menschen.

World Bank (1994): *Averting the Old Age Crisis. Policies to Protect the Old and Promote Growth.* Washington, DC: Oxford University Press.

World Bank (2001): *Pension Reform: Technical Assistance Mission.* AIDE-MEMOIRE, internal material MPSV.

Chapter 4
Between State and Market: Czech and Slovene Pension Reform in Comparison

Katharina Müller[1]

In marked contrast with recent moves towards pension privatisation in several post-socialist countries, policymakers in the Czech Republic and Slovenia have so far dismissed a radical reform of old-age security. Instead, they embarked on a series of parametric reforms, while complementing their public pay-as-you-go (PAYG) scheme with a voluntary private tier. This chapter sets out to compare the observable policy outcomes in the Czech Republic and Slovenia. After summarising their pre-war and socialist legacy, the political, economic and demographic context in which the Czech and Slovene reforms occurred is discussed comparatively. Thereafter the pension reform measures taken over the past decade are reviewed in greater detail. Starting out from the relevant literature on the political economy of pension reform, the subsequent sections seek to come up with a comparative explanation of the paradigm choice of Czech and Slovene policymakers against the policy recommendations of the 'new pension orthodoxy'.

The legacy
When designing their post-socialist pension reform strategies, Czech and Slovene policymakers did not start from scratch, but set out to rebuild the already existing institutional framework. While exhibiting similar traits in all formerly socialist countries, the pre-1990 pension schemes were not identical. In the case of the Czech Republic and Slovenia, the common legacy predates the decades of socialist rule, as both found themselves governed by the Habsburg monarchy until 1918. It was during this period that the first old-age security schemes were introduced. While pensions for civil servants and teachers were introduced in the late 18th

---
[1] European University Viadrina, Frankfurt (Oder)

century, miners and railway workers had to wait until the second half of the 19th century. A generalised scheme for clerks was only introduced in 1906 (see De Deken, 1994: 4–6). In the Czechoslovak Republic manual workers received generalised pension protection in 1924, whereas in the Kingdom of Yugoslavia a universal old-age insurance was introduced in 1937. These early pension schemes were clearly inspired by the Bismarckian pension insurance of 1889 (e.g. in their differential treatment for white- and blue-collar workers), but they were introduced decades later and in a piecemeal fashion.

After World War II, the existing pension schemes underwent fundamental change. In Czechoslovakia, the fragmented pension schemes were unified in 1948, while a unification of the Yugoslav old-age insurance scheme had already occurred in the interwar period. During communist rule, the Czechoslovak pension scheme was more closely modelled on the Soviet example than the Yugoslav one. In 1952, it was integrated into the state budget and financed entirely out of tax revenues. All occupations were classified into three labour categories, with a bias towards manual workers in heavy industry. The latter were granted higher benefit levels and early retirement, thus marking an important departure from universalism. In 'deviationist' Yugoslavia, however, Soviet features in old-age provision, such as (explicit) labour categories, did not last long. Instead, its character as a Federal Republic came to be reflected in the organisation of social security. Contributory financing was restored, and by the mid-1950s, individual social insurance institutes were set up in each of the republics, with separate funds by branches of social security. In both countries, the retirement age was set at 60 for men, while for women, it was age 55 (Yugoslavia) and ages 53–57 (Czechoslovakia). With the surge of inflation in the 1980s, the insufficient adjustment of current pensions to inflation gave rise to problems of inter-cohort fairness and benefit adequacy. Yugoslav and Czechoslovak policymakers reacted by enacting indexation laws in 1982 and 1988, respectively. In 1989, net replacement rates reached 63.8 percent in Czechoslovakia and as much as 80 percent in Slovenia (see Mácha and Stanovnik, this volume).

The context
In 1990, after the first multiparty elections since World War II, Yugoslavia and Czechoslovakia were not only heading towards a new political and economic system, but also towards the break-up of their confederations: Slovenia declared independence from Yugoslavia in June 1991, and the Czech and Slovak Republics separated in January 1993. Hence, in both the Czech Republic and Slovenia,

economic and political transformation had to be handled simultaneously with the consolidation of a nation-state, a challenge referred to as 'triple transition' (Offe, 1994: 64–65). After a decade of transition, Slovenia and the Czech Republic are now among the most advanced post-socialist countries and are awaiting early accession to the European Union (see EBRD, 2001a, b). Both countries have stable and well-functioning democratic institutions, and Eurostat data show that they have consistently exhibited the highest GDP per capita (in PPS) among the post-socialist Candidate Countries. In 1997, Slovenia surpassed Greece, which has the EU-minimum in terms of GDP per capita. The country has now reached 71 percent of the EU-15 average, while the Czech Republic saw its comparative percentage slashed from 65 to 58 percent following economic crisis (see Stapel, 2001).

Table 1
Slovenia: Selected economic indicators, 1993–2000

	1993	1994	1995	1996	1997	1998	1999	2000
GDP at constant prices (% change)	2.8	5.3	4.1	3.5	4.6	3.8	5.0	4.3
Inflation (annual average % change)	32.3	19.8	12.6	9.7	9.1	7.9	6.1	8.9
General gov't balance (% of GDP)	0.9	0.0	0.0	0.3	-1.2	-0.8	-0.6	-1.4
Unemployment (% of labour force)	9.1	9.1	7.4	7.3	7.4	7.9	7.6	7.2
External debt stock (US$ billions)	1.9	2.3	3.0	4.0	4.2	5.0	5.5	5.8
– % of GDP	na	15.7	15.8	21.2	22.9	25.4	27.9	26.8
External debt service (% of exports)	na	5.3	6.8	8.5	8.5	13.2	7.7	10.3

Source: EBRD (2001c); World Bank (2000).

Note: For debt indicators, 1998 and 1999 data are estimates. For all other indicators, 2000 data are estimates (projections for debt data).

In political terms, Slovenia has been dominated by the centre-left LDS since independence, with the exception of a brief period between June and November 2000, during which the Slovenes had a centre-right government. While the LDS won a plurality of seats in parliament in the 1992 elections, it joined a coalition with three smaller parties. In 1996 it emerged as the country's strongest party without receiving an overall majority of seats. After lengthy negotiations, the LDS formed an alliance with the rightist People's Party and the Pensioners' Party to achieve a comfortable majority of seats. In the Czech Republic, coalitions led by

Václav Klaus' centre-right party, the ODS, governed the country throughout most of the 1990s, favouring liberal economic policy. After enjoying a parliamentary majority from 1992 to 1996, Klaus's coalition lost its majority by a narrow margin in the 1996 parliamentary elections. His minority government only survived until 1997, and after a short-lived caretaker government, the major opposition party, the Social Democrats, won the elections in 1998, albeit so narrowly that they installed a minority government tolerated by the ODS. Hence, in both countries, the political conditions in the second half of the 1990s may have been less than propitious for pursuing radical reform. Due to the broad character of the coalition in Slovenia, the need to embark on consensus-building prevailed, while successive minority governments in the Czech Republic seemed to allow for very little leeway in policymaking.[2]

As all transition countries, the Czech Republic and Slovenia faced a decline in real GDP in the immediate aftermath of the economic regime change, averaging -6.1 and -7.2 percent in 1991–92, respectively (see EBRD, 2001a). Table 1 and 2 show, however, that both economies swiftly recovered from 1993 onwards. In Slovenia, the steady rates of economic growth have been continuing until the present day, averaging 4.2 percent over the past eight years. These economic dynamics enabled the country to outperform all other transition countries in terms of GDP per capita. The unemployment rate has fallen by 1.9 percent since 1993 and reached 7.2 percent in 2000, while inflation remained high at a biannual average of 7.5 percent (1999–2000). Over the past four years, a small fiscal deficit has developed. The Czech Republic was long seen as the front-runner in economic transition. Economic growth averaged 1.4 percent over the past eight years, but the country experienced an economic downturn in 1997–99 (see Table 2). Triggered by current account deficits and speculative attacks on the Czech currency, the crisis is now widely attributed to a lack of financial sector and capital market reform. In the aftermath, the notoriously low unemployment rates more than doubled and reached 9.4 percent in 1999. In the wake of economic stabilisation, inflation rates decreased considerably, reaching a biannual average of 3 percent (1999–2000). At the same time the fiscal deficit, that had been low in the years following 1994, took an upward turn and peaked at 4.8 percent in 2000.

---

[2] Strong governments do not always embark on radical reform either, as concentrated authority is tantamount to concentrated responsibility, providing little chance of blame avoidance (see Pierson, 1996).

Table 2
Czech Republic: Selected economic indicators, 1993–2000

	1993	1994	1995	1996	1997	1998	1999	2000
GDP at constant prices (% change)	0.1	2.2	5.9	4.8	-1.0	-2.2	-0.8	2.5
Inflation (annual average % change)	20.8	9.9	9.1	8.8	8.5	10.7	2.1	3.9
General gov't balance (% of GDP)	0.5	-1.1	-1.4	-0.9	-1.7	-2.0	-3.3	-4.8
Unemployment (% of labour force)	3.5	3.2	2.9	3.5	5.2	7.5	9.4	8.8
External debt stock (US$ billions)	8.5	10.7	16.6	20.9	21.4	24.1	22.6	23.0
– % of GDP	28.2	28.9	33.1	36.8	44.9	40.4	45.1	43.0
External debt service (% of exports)	na	13.1	9.2	10.7	15.6	15.1	12.5	na

Source: EBRD (2001b); World Bank (2001a).

Note: 2000 data are projections.

In both countries, external debt has tripled since 1993 (see Tables 1 and 2). However, 86 percent of the Slovene debt was contracted with private creditors, not with bilateral or multilateral agencies, and so was 60 percent of the Czech debt. In the Czech Republic, more than a quarter of the total external debt was short-term, rendering the Czech economy more vulnerable to international capital movements (see World Bank, 2001b, 2001c). According to World Bank classifications,[3] the Czech Republic is an upper-middle income, less indebted country (see World Bank, 2001d). As pointed out in World Bank (2001a: 13), the Czech Republic even has a net *creditor* position vis-á-vis the outside world. In turn, Slovenia is classified as high income and will soon graduate from World Bank financial and technical assistance altogether (see World Bank, 2000). International country ratings indicate that Slovenia and the Czech Republic currently enjoy the best evaluation of all transition countries in terms of investment risk and credit rating.[4] Still, in 1989–2000 the scale of foreign direct

---

[3] For the year 2000, the following thresholds for GNI per capita were in place, following the World Bank Atlas method: low income, US$ 755 or less; lower middle income, US$ 756 to 2,995; upper middle income, US$ 2,996 to 9,265; high income, US$ 9,266 or more (World Bank, 2001: 335).

[4] As of March 2000, composite ICRG risk rating was 76.3 and 79.8 in the Czech Republic and Slovenia, respectively (regional average: 63.7), while the Institutional Investor credit rating was 59.1 and 63.1, respectively (regional average: 27.5). See World Bank (2001d: 306–307).

investment (FDI) differed considerably: with US$ 1,884 of cumulative FDI inflows per capita, the Czech Republic ranks second among all post-socialist countries, while Slovenia reached only US$ 768 (see EBRD, 2001a).

Although state capacity is hard to measure, Slovenia and the Czech Republic have been graded among the best post-socialist performers (see Bönker, 2001). In terms of tax effectiveness, both countries outperformed all other transition countries in the period 1996–98. With 43.0 and 39.3 percent of GDP, respectively, the level of general government revenues was still high, and Slovenia and the Czech Republic ranked third and sixth among the transition countries with regard to this indicator. Both countries exhibit a comparatively low level of state capture (see Hellman, Jones and Kaufmann, 2000: 9). Yet, the Capture Economy Index is higher for the Czech Republic (11) than for Slovenia (7), and so is administrative corruption: while Central-Eastern European firms pay an average of 2.2 percent of annual revenues p.a. in unofficial payments to public officials, Slovene firms pay 1.4 percent and Czech firms 2.5 percent.[5] Organisations such as the EU Commission, the EBRD and the World Bank recommend the continuation of efforts to restructure and privatise state-owned enterprises and to improve corporate governance and the performance of regulatory agencies, especially in the banking and financial sector.[6] In the Czech Republic in particular, non-performing loans averaged 34 percent of total loans in the period 1994–98, similar to the ratios in Romania or Slovakia (see World Bank, 2001a: 4).[7]

---

[5] '*State capture* is defined as shaping the formation of the basic rules of the game (i.e. laws, rules, decrees and regulations) through illicit and non-transparent private payments to public officials.... *Administrative corruption* is defined as private payments to public officials to distort the prescribed implementation of official rules and policies' (see Hellman, Jones and Kaufmann, 2000: 2; italics by K. M.). See also Hellman and Kaufmann (2001).

[6] For these recommendations see, e.g., EBRD (2001b, 2001c), World Bank (2000, 2001).

[7] In Slovenia, non-performing loans averaged 4 percent in 1994–98 (see World Bank, 2001: 4).

Table 3
Selected demographic indicators, 1999-2015

	Population under age 15 (as % of total)		Population above age 64 (as % of total)		Total fertility rate (per woman)	
	1999	2015	1999	2015	1999	2015
Slovenia	16.4	11.9	13.6	18.6	2.2	1.2
Czech Republic	16.8	12.8	13.7	18.7	2.2	1.2
Eastern Europe & FSU	21.4	15.9	11.5	12.9	2.5	1.5

Source: UNDP (2001)

Note: 2015 data refer to medium-variant projections.

Over the past decade, Slovenia and the Czech Republic have been the highest ranking post-socialist countries in terms of the Human Development Index, calculated by the UNDP.[8] Among all transition countries, they enjoyed the highest life expectancy at birth (1999: 75.3 and 74.7 years, respectively) and had the highest probability at birth of surviving to age 60 (see UNDP, 2001). Hence, it is not surprising that Slovenia and the Czech Republic also surpass the post-socialist countries' average in terms of population ageing, both current and projected (see Table 3). Even if in 1999, their share of population aged 65 and above was lower than in Croatia, Estonia, Hungary and Bulgaria, in 2015 they are bound to outdo all other countries in the region. Both countries already have a very low share of under 15-year-olds, beaten only by Bulgaria. In terms of fertility, they are closer to the regional average, which is expected to fall below replacement in the coming years. Yet total population decrease is likely to be partially offset in Slovenia and the Czech Republic, as they are currently enjoying the highest rates of net migration among the post-socialist Candidate Countries (see Eurostat, 2001: 2).

---

[8] The dimensions of human development measured in the Human Development Index are GDP per capita (PPP US$), life expectancy at birth, adult literacy, and combined primary, secondary and tertiary gross enrolment (see UNDP, 2001: 240).

Old-age security in transformation

Economic transformation affected the existing public pension systems in the Czech Republic and Slovenia in several ways. Price liberalisation and the curtailment of subsidies on basic goods and services required a shift from indirect to direct transfers, resulting in rising expenditures for old-age security. The restructuring and privatisation of state-owned enterprises had an effect on both the revenue and the expenditure side of public pension schemes, as it was accompanied by a mounting number of disability pensions and by early retirement policies. Designed to avoid large-scale unemployment, these policies led to an increased number of pensioners and a falling number of contributors to the schemes (see Mácha and Stanovnik, this volume). In Slovenia, the number of insured persons per pensioner fell from 2.30 (1990) to 1.71 (1993) and 1.67 (2000); in the Czech Republic, it decreased from 2.00 (1993) to 1.80 (2000). Since the respective old-age dependency ratios remained largely unchanged over the same period, it is clear that the immediate threat to the financial viability of the existing pension schemes in Slovenia and the Czech Republic was transformation-induced rather than stemming from population ageing (but cf. Table 3 for future demographic perspectives).

Both Slovenia and the Czech Republic exhibited mounting levels of pension expenditure over the past decade (see Mácha and Stanovnik, this volume). The Slovene pension expenditures rose from 10.9 percent of GDP (1991) to 14.1 per cent (1993) and 14.6 per cent (2000), i.e. by 34 per cent in 1990–2000 and by a mere 4 per cent since 1993.[9] In the Czech Republic, 1993 pension expenditure amounted to only half of the Slovene figure in 1993 (7.2 per cent of GDP), yet by 2000 it had risen to 9.6 per cent, i.e. by 33 per cent. Consequently, increasing transfers from the state budget were necessary to cover pension expenditures. While the Slovene Institute for Pension and Disability Insurance relied on budgetary transfers throughout the whole decade, the level of these transfers rose more than four-fold in the period 1994–2000.[10] The Czech Social Insurance Administration, financially

---

[9] The Slovene figures on pension expenditures used here seem to be above the EU-15 average calculated by Eurostat (12.6 percent of GDP in 1998). Yet following the Eurostat methodology, the Slovene expenditures only amount to 12 percent and are thus slightly below the EU-15 figure (see Amerini, 2001).

[10] Up to 1996, budgetary transfers made by the Slovene government were limited to non-insurance benefits disbursed by the Institute for Pension and Disability Insurance (see Stanovnik, this volume).

integrated into the state budget, exhibited a soaring deficit from 1997 onwards, after the contribution rate had been lowered from 27.2 to 26 percent in 1996.

While comparability is limited by the fact that Czech data prior to 1993 are unavailable, these figures suggest that in Slovenia the major hike in pension expenditures occurred in the early 1990s, when the country faced a substantial drop in the insured/pensioner ratio.[11] In comparison, the Czech Republic faced the brunt of this double dynamics only in the second half of the 1990s, after economic crisis had pushed unemployment rates up (see Table 2). The pressure to reform the old-age security scheme in Slovenia was also higher because the net replacement rate peaked at 89.2 percent of wages in 1990, while still reaching 76.1 percent in 2000. In the Czech Republic, it amounted to 65.2 (1990) and 57.2 percent in 2000 (see Mácha and Stanovnik, this volume). On the other hand, Tables 1 and 2 have shown that throughout the past decade, Slovenia enjoyed more fiscal leeway than the Czech Republic and could therefore 'afford' larger fiscal transfers to its pension scheme.

When economic and political transformation started, social security experts and policymakers in both Slovenia and the Czech Republic realised that the old-age security systems inherited from the socialist past were in need of reform, both to secure their financial sustainability and to adapt some of the previous design features to the new economic order. The reforms they prepared essentially focused on their public PAYG schemes (see Table 4): a gradual increase in pensionable age, a tightening of eligibility, a restriction of access to early retirement and to invalidity pensions, the abolition of branch privileges in the Czech Republic and their transformation into employer-financed, pre-funded regimes in Slovenia. In the Czech Republic, contributory financing was reintroduced in 1993, with contributions split among pension, sickness and unemployment insurance, as well as between employers and employees.[12] Whereas in Slovenia both contributory financing and an autonomous pension institute were already in place well before independence, the separation of Czech pension finances from the state budget has

---

[11] Stanovnik (this volume) argues that the subsequent stabilisation of the insured/pensioner ratio was only achieved by including 'marginal' contributors into the system.

[12] Even if dividing the contribution burden is largely irrelevant in economic terms, East European reformers found it important to introduce individualised contributions as part of a more general agenda towards self-provision and insurance-type arrangements, 'after decades of spoon-feeding' (Kornai, 1997: 1186).

so far proven impossible. Although a special account within the state budget was created to earmark pension surpluses for future deficits, this was shortly before pension finances went into the red and could only have helped to increase public awareness of the pension scheme's financial difficulties. When policymakers made an effort to lower labour costs, decreasing the contribution burden by 1.7 percent (Czech Republic) and 8.85 percent (Slovenia), they heightened the schemes' dependency on budgetary transfers.

In Slovenia, two major legislative efforts to fix the PAYG system stand out – the Pension and Disability Insurance Acts of 1992 and 1999. While the former mainly introduced stricter eligibility rules, a reaction to soaring pension expenditures, the 1999 Act followed four years of substantial negotiations, both within the ruling coalition and with social partners. It introduced a system of penalties and bonuses for early and delayed retirement, increased the pensionable age for women, decreased accrual rates and further tightened eligibility. In the Czech Republic, the Klaus government obtained parliamentary approval for a very controversial Pension Insurance Act in 1995, that introduced a two-part pension formula and raised the retirement age. Contrary to this, the Social Democrats' recent plans to embark on a more substantial reform of the PAYG system, possibly including the introduction of a notional defined contribution (NDC)[13] scheme, remained stalled for a lack of political consensus. It even proved impossible to increase contribution rates from 26 to 28.4 percent to correct the pension scheme's most immediate financial imbalances.

In addition to such parametric reforms intended to improve the financial viability of the public PAYG schemes, policymakers in many transition countries decided to change the public-private mix in old-age provision. By introducing supplementary schemes on a voluntary basis, self-provision for old age was to be strengthened. Furthermore, the newly licensed pension funds were expected to provide long-term investment capital, thereby contributing to the development of the local capital markets. This model was followed in the Czech Republic (see Table 5). In 1994, a law establishing supplementary private pension funds was approved by Parliament, the incentive to fund members being a nominally fixed state

---

[13] In a NDC scheme, all contribution payments are recorded in notional individualised accounts, yet capital accumulation is only virtual. Individual benefit levels depend mainly on past contributions and their notional rate of return. The latter is a discretionary factor, boiling down to an indexation of the virtual pension capital to the growth in the contribution base. Moreover, future benefit amounts are linked to cohort mortality trends and the chosen retirement age. Designed by Swedish reformers, NDC schemes were pioneered in Latvia and Poland (see Müller, 2002).

Table 4
Basic features of the public pension schemes in the Czech Republic and Slovenia

Characteristics	Czech Republic	Slovenia
Type	mandatory, PAYG	mandatory, PAYG
Nominal contribution rate	26.0	24.35
– of which employees	6.5	15.50
– of which employers	19.5	8.85
Contribution ceiling	no	no
Separation of pension fund from state budget	no, but specially earmarked account	yes, autonomous pension insurance institute
Structure of pension formula	flat-rate basic part + earnings-related component	benefit calculation based on individual wage history and contributory years
Minimum insurance period	25	15
Earnings considered in pension base	last 30 years (2016)	average of best 18 year
Pensionable age after transition period (men/women)	62/57–61	65/63*
Bonuses for late retirement	yes	yes
Penalties for early retirement	yes	yes, if prior to age 61/63 (with many exceptions)
Branch privileges	abolished	transformed into separate contributory funded tier

Sources: Mácha and Stanovnik (this volume); Müller (1999)
* For a pension qualifying period of 20 years and above, the full pensionable age is 63/61 (men/women).

subsidy. Václav Klaus, inspired by Thatcherite social policy and an outspoken critic of corporatism, had pushed for this individualistic approach. A proposal by the Ministry of Labour and Social Affairs, supported by trade unions and employees' associations, to introduce occupational pension schemes as in Continental Europe was dismissed. Yet, although the number of private pension funds mushroomed, peaking at 44 in 1995–96, the amount of voluntary contributions collected fell short of expectations. In 2000, with 43 percent of the labour force participating in the nineteen remaining pension funds, total assets amounted to a mere 2.3 percent of GDP. This is mainly due to the fact that on average, participants spend only around 3 percent of the average wage on monthly contributions (see Mácha, this volume). After amendments effective from January 2000 more generous tax incentives are in place, yet whether this will produce a significant effect on assets and fund membership still remains to be seen.

The Slovene approach to supplementary old-age provision proved to be more heterodox. While a supplementary scheme was introduced as early as 1992, it was run under the auspices of the Institute for Pension and Disability Insurance, albeit with a separation of assets. This public monopoly did not manage to attract more than a few hundred Slovenes, given the absence of tax incentives. In late 1999, the market was eventually opened to private providers of collective and individual old-age schemes, leading to a coexistence of employer-sponsored occupational schemes and individualist personal pension arrangements (see Table 5).

Table 5
Basic features of the voluntary supplementary funds
in the Czech Republic and Slovenia*

Characteristics	Czech Republic	Slovenia
Year of introduction	1994	2000
Financing	fully-funded	fully-funded
Types of pension plans offered	personal	personal or occupational
Corporate constitution	Joint Stock Companies	Joint Stock Companies or Mutual Funds
Government incentives	state subsidy and tax incentives	tax incentives
Employers' contribution	tax-exempt (with ceiling)	tax-exempt (with ceiling)
Supervision	Ministry of Finance	Insurance Supervision Agency or Securities Market Agency
Number of funds	18	15
Number of members (thousands)	2,281	40
Members in % of population	22.3	0.02
Total assets (% of GDP)	2.3	na

Sources: Mácha and Stanovnik (this volume); Müller (1999)
* Here, only the competitive supplementary schemes are covered, i.e. both the state-run 'First Pension Fund' and the monolithic supplementary scheme introduced in 1992 are left out of consideration.

Depending on their corporate design as mutual funds or as pension management companies, they are subject to supervision from either the Securities Market Agency or the Insurance Supervision Agency. The new law provides for a minimum rate of return guarantee and generous tax incentives for employers and fund members. By mid-2001 fourteen funds with about 40,000 members had been set up, and these are successfully competing with KAD, the successor of the statist fund, now managed by the Pension Management Fund, *Kapitalska družba* (see Stanovnik, this volume).

Two other supplementary pension schemes, also managed by *Kapitalska družba* , were introduced by different pieces of 1999 legislation.[14] One is a mandatory supplementary scheme, covering those insured involved in particularly hard and unhealthy work, or performing activities which cannot be continued after attaining a certain age. To allow for the early retirement of these insured, previous legislation had obliged employers to pay increased contributions to the Institute for Pension and Disability Insurance. The amount above the normal contribution rate is now capitalised at *Kapitalska družba*, making this special group of insured eligible for early retirement pensions from the supplementary scheme. The other new pension scheme is run by the so-called 'First Pension Fund', which is also managed by *Kapitalska družba*. It is a voluntary scheme, allowing Slovenes to swap their remaining ownership certificates from privatisation for pension coupons. While the original proposal involved an automatic swap of ownership certificates, the law made the swap optional and also introduced a per capita limit of ownership certificates to be traded in. Therefore, only 5 percent of the total value of the remaining ownership certificates has been allotted to the First Pension Fund so far (see Stanovnik, this volume).[15]

The paradigm choice made in the Czech Republic and Slovenia remained well

---

[14] It is interesting to note that both of these rather unconventional schemes also feature in the recent Bulgarian pension reform, with a greater role for private providers. The mandatory supplementary scheme for the formerly privileged occupations started operations in early 2001, yet it is based on competing private funds. The Bulgarian law also allows to transfer privatisation vouchers to specialised pension funds, but private providers have so far be unwilling to set up the respective funds, as they are not interested in this business (cf. Chiappe, 2001; Nikolov, 2001).

[15] For a discussion of alternative links between pension reform and the privatisation of state-owned enterprises see Gesell-Schmidt, Müller and Süß (1999).

within the boundaries of the Bismarckian welfare paradigm, with some Beveridgean flavour in the Czech pension formula. Whereas the Slovene case exhibits features of path-dependency, showing a strong tendency to perpetuate the Yugoslav social insurance model, the Czech reforms can be interpreted as a reinvention of the pre-communist welfare state traditions (see Hartl and Večerník 1992: 161). Even though both the Czech Republic and Slovenia faced an intense debate about the need for a privately managed and fully-funded mandatory tier (see Mácha and Stanovnik, this volume), the cautious pension reform path followed by successive governments remained unchanged. Starting from the existing body of knowledge on radical reforms and their absence, not only in the area of pensions, the next sections will seek to explain which structural-institutional and actor-related factors accounted for both the emergence of proposals to privatise Czech and Slovene old-age security and for their eventual dismissal by relevant policymakers.

Explaining pension reform choices: foreign influence, local actors and the policy context

This section is largely based on the literature on the political economy of policy reform, published over the past decade.[16] This multi-disciplinary strand of research analyses the factors enabling or restricting the viability of radical, market-oriented reforms. More specifically, it draws on recent work on the political economy of pension reform.[17] The heuristics is inspired by actor-centred institutionalism, a methodology that seeks to overcome the 'classical' schism within social sciences (Mayntz and Scharpf, 1995; Scharpf, 1997).

---

[16] For an overview on the political economy of policy reform see Rodrik (1996), Tommasi and Velasco (1996), Sturzenegger and Tommasi (1998), Drazen (2000), and Krueger (2000).

[17] See Müller (1999), Cain (2000), Cashu (2000a, b), Orenstein (2000), and Nelson (2001) for the post-socialist countries; Kay (1998, 1999), Madrid (1999, 2002), Mesa-Lago (1999), Mora (1999), Busquets (2000), Huber and Stephens (2000), and Mesa-Lago and Müller (2002) for Latin America; and Brooks (1998, 2001), Madrid (1998, 2001), Chłoń and Mora (2001), James and Brooks (2001), Müller (2001), and Orenstein (2001) for a cross-regional explanatory framework.

The 'new pension orthodoxy'

In many Latin American and East European countries, the public-private mix in mandatory pension provision has been changed significantly over the past decade. The recent wave of full or partial pension privatisation, i.e. the adoption of similar blueprints across countries and regions, suggests a common international transmission mechanism of ideas. And indeed, a dominant epistemic community[18] can clearly be identified: a 'new pension orthodoxy' (Lo Vuolo, 1996) has been giving major impulses to pension privatisation in Latin America and Eastern Europe, arguing that such paradigm change in old-age security would lead to both a rise in saving and to efficiency improvements in financial and labour markets, thereby resulting in an increase in long-term growth (see, e.g. Corsetti and Schmidt-Hebbel, 1997).

Conservative critics of the welfare state had long prepared the ground for a paradigm change in old-age security, as described by Hirschman (1991). It was in the wake of the end of the cold war that the terms of the prevailing discourse in old-age protection shifted, interacting with the rise of neoliberalism as the dominant paradigm in economic policymaking, particularly in developing and transition countries. While originally not contained in the so-called 'Washington Consensus' (Williamson 1990, 2000), pension privatisation has since become part and parcel of the neoliberal reform package by now. In Eastern Europe, this paradigm shift coincided with the first post-socialist years, marked by a widespread move towards the market in economic policy.

An increasing amount of contemporary policy change is affected by policy transfer and the global diffusion of models (see Dolowitz and Marsh, 2000; Weyland, 2000). Radical agenda shifting in old-age security reform was frequently associated with World Bank involvement. In 1994, the Bank's research report on pension policy attracted global attention (see World Bank, 1994). The best-known exemplification of what has become the 'new pension orthodoxy', it was also its major propagating mechanism.[19] Apart from the ubiquitous condition-

---

[18] An epistemic community is a network of professionals in a particular domain and with a common policy enterprise, who may come from different professional backgrounds. They share faith in specific truths and in a set of normative and causal beliefs, have shared patterns of reasoning and use shared discursive practices (see Adler and Haas, 1992; Haas, 1992).

[19] A sizeable 'heterodoxy' remains, however. Mesa-Lago (1996) and Ney (2000) point to conflicting policy prescriptions by international organisations. For the debate between the World Bank and the ILO see Beattie and McGillivray (1995) and James (1996). For a recent critique of the 'new pension orthodoxy' see Barr (2000), Charlton and McKinnon (2001), Orszag and Stiglitz (2001).

alities, channels to support pension privatisation include loans and an expert-based knowledge transfer – a potentially attractive assistance package for local policymakers. In recent years other international financial institutions and government agencies – such as the International Monetary Fund (IMF) and the US Agency for International Development (USAID) – have followed suit. Although they have taken part in relevant cross-conditionalities with the Bank, as well as other forms of co-operation, overall they play a less outstanding role.

Earlier research has made it clear, however, that in order to be adopted in the local reform arena, the new orthodox template requires not only an agent for its transmission, but also an influential local actor ready to adopt neoliberal blueprints, generally the Ministry of Finance (see Müller, 1999). Full or partial pension privatisation became feasible when those actors inclined towards pension privatisation – the Ministry of Finance and the World Bank – had stakes and leverage in the local reform process. By comparison, radical pension reform did not proceed when the Welfare Ministry was the only relevant pension reform actor.

The pension reform arena: actors and constraints
While the full or partial privatisation of old-age security was clearly a major policy recommendation from abroad facing any pension reformer in Eastern Europe, it was the domestic political process that eventually resulted in the adoption or rejection of radical pension reform. The following analysis includes the identification of relevant political actors in the pension reform arena and the consideration of the policy context that shaped their room for manœuvre, influenced by political factors and economic conditions.

Scholars of the political economy of policy reform have stressed the importance of political leadership – courageous, committed individuals, often market-oriented economists – and their ability to communicate a coherent neoliberal vision (see Harberger, 1993; Sachs, 1994). It has been shown elsewhere that pension privatisation amounts to a paradigm shift that may be greatly facilitated by such committed policymakers. However, the existence of these agenda setters can certainly not be considered sufficient to guarantee success against powerful interest groups (see Williamson and Haggard, 1994; Tommasi and Velasco, 1996).

As noted above, radical paradigm change in old-age security has been advocated mainly by the Ministry of Finance, staffed with neoliberally trained economists. This alliance of players, together with the Ministry of Economic Affairs and the Central Bank, felt that pension privatisation perfectly matched their overall efforts to decrease the role of the state in the economy. These local advocates of a globally propagated agenda were supported both by local interest groups, such as business organisations and the financial sector, and the international financial institutions. But there was also opposition to these radical plans, both within and outside government. More often than not, the Ministries of Labour, Welfare or Health, responsible for the existing old-age security schemes, were reluctant to engage in structural pension reform, thus reflecting the existing Bismarckian traditions in Eastern Europe. In several countries, these Ministries initially objected to the radical paradigm shift, but – given the predominance of the Finance Ministry in the cabinet – proved too weak to prevent it. Typically, the Labour Ministry's influence on reform design was deliberately limited by the setting up of small task forces, mostly attached to the Ministry of Finance. These special pension reform committees worked out the draft legislation and served to bypass the Labour Ministry's pension-related competences (see Müller, 1999; Nelson, 2001).

Other local opponents of pension privatisation included trade unions, social security employees, and – last but not least – pensioners' associations and special interest groups with privileged pension schemes. In several countries, left-wing parties also joined the ranks of opponents. Clearly, the specific policy context may provide reformers or reform opponents with action resources (see Kay, 1999). The executive's degree of control of the legislature amounts to a pivotal institutional variable. Veto points, built into the political system, provide a particular group with strategic opportunities and potential political impact (see Immergut, 1992). In some countries trade unions had traditional ties with the governing parties that were used to ease resistance. Yet these ties also implied that reform opponents were in a political position that forced pension reformers to negotiate and to make concessions, most notably granting trade unions the right to run their own pension funds (see Isuani and San Martino, 1998; Orenstein, 2000).

Economic factors and considerations appear to have had a substantial impact on the choice of reform model. As noted above, pension privatisation has been primarily proposed for macroeconomic motives, seeking to embark on a virtuous circle leading to economic growth. Madrid (1998) and James and Brooks (2001) have pointed to increased international capital mobility and the recent experiences of capital market crises, that may have induced policymakers to seek to reduce the vulnerability to capital outflows by boosting domestic savings and the local capital market.[20] Moreover, scholars of the political economy of policy reform have highlighted that a preceding crisis may induce radical change – the so-called 'benefit of crises' hypothesis (see Drazen and Grilli, 1993).[21] Fiscal crises turn the Ministry of Finance into a potential actor in the pension reform arena. More specifically, when pension financing goes into deficit, the resulting dependence on budgetary subsidies grant this likely advocate of the 'new pension orthodoxy' an important stake in reforming old-age security (see Müller, 1999). Furthermore, a persistent financial crisis may severely erode public confidence in the public pension systems, thus facilitating fundamental reform.

Yet another economic factor had an impact on the cases of pension reform reviewed above: when external debt is high, governments tend to stress their general commitment to market-oriented reform. In this context, the announcement of pension privatisation can be interpreted as a 'signalling' strategy (cf. Rodrik, 1998). And indeed, by the mid-1990s, rating agencies had included radical pension reform as a point in favour in their country-risk assessments. Critical indebtedness also increases the likelihood of the involvement of international financial institutions in the local pension reform arena (see Brooks, 1998). Their leverage is partially determined by their stakes as important creditors in many transition countries. However, their impact is not limited to binding conditionalities resulting from their own financial involvement. Rather, it is the general level of external indebtedness that matters, as the IMF and the World Bank 'may signal that a developing country has embraced sound policies and hence boost its credibility' (Stiglitz, 1998: 27). When their recommendations are disregarded by local governments, alternative sources of market financing are often hard to obtain. As noted by Kay (1999), policymakers were well aware that financial and/or technical support from the international financial institutions was only available for a pension reform that included a privatisation component.

---

[20] Yet, contrary to these high hopes, the Chilean evidence suggests that pension privatisation actually had a negative impact on national saving (see Mesa-Lago, 1998).

[21] Situations of perceived emergency can induce contending political groups to agree upon unpopular, painful measures and facilitate the destruction of political coalitions that had blocked reform, breaking a previously existing stalemate (see Williamson, 1994). However, the 'benefit of crises' hypothesis has not met with unanimity among scholars of the political economy of policy reform.

Earlier scholarship on welfare state development has stressed the importance of existing institutional arrangements for future reform paths – policy feedback or path dependence.[22] 'Existing policies can set the agenda for change ... by narrowing the range of feasible alternatives' (Pierson and Weaver, 1993: 146). Frequently, the success of reform strategies depends on earlier policy choices and the policy feedback resulting from them. In Bismarckian-style PAYG schemes, lock-in effects and opportunity costs may result from the pension rights earned by the insured, engendering high transition costs. The size of these entitlements, frequently called 'implicit pension debt', is determined by a number of factors, notably the percentage of the population covered, the maturity of the scheme and the generosity of benefits. When made explicit, it translates into high fiscal costs. It has therefore been argued that the larger the implicit pension debt, the smaller the likelihood for the most radical structural pension reform (see James and Brooks, 2001).

The dismissal of pension privatisation in the Czech Republic and Slovenia
Today, the pension system in both the Czech Republic and Slovenia is essentially two-tiered, combining a public mandatory PAYG scheme with a supplementary funded tier. While the second tier[23] in the Czech Republic consists of a voluntary private scheme offering personal pension plans, there are three supplementary pension schemes in Slovenia: a voluntary private scheme that can take the form of occupational schemes or personal pension plans, as well as a mandatory scheme for the formerly privileged branches and a pension fund for privatisation certificates, both run by the state-owned *Kapitalska družba*. Unlike in other post-socialist states, there has been no shift to funding at the expense of the public pension tier in either country. Why did pension privatisation not succeed in the Czech and Slovene context?

The Czech case
Until the mid-1990s, the basic conflict surrounding pension reform in the Czech Republic had been about the scope of parametric reform. Advocates of full or partial pension privatisation made themselves heard shortly afterwards: young

---

[22] On the concept of policy feedback see Esping-Andersen (1985) and Pierson (1993); for a recent discussion of the concept of path dependence see Pierson (2000).
[23] According to World Bank terminology, this would be a third-pillar scheme (see, e.g., World Bank, 1994).

Czech economists with connections to the international orthodoxy – 'market komsomols' in local jargon – had joined forces with the stakeholders from the financial community and the liberal Union of Freedom to place pension privatisation on the political agenda (see e.g. Schneider, 1996a, b; Jelínek and Schneider, 1997a, b). Moreover, the concomitant pension reform efforts of other countries in the region, notably Hungary and Poland, did not go unnoticed in the Czech Republic. However, the efforts at agenda-shifting did not succeed in having an impact on the overall reform strategy pursued by the Czech government. After simulating the overall impact and costs related to a partial privatisation of the Czech pension scheme, as against the alternative, a thorough reform of the existing PAYG scheme, the experts at the Ministry of Labour concluded that there was still sufficient leeway within the existing public PAYG system to face the challenges of the next decades (see Mácha, this volume).

The World Bank, the main transmitter of the 'new pension orthodoxy', could have reinforced the local privatisation faction with its global experience in promoting and assisting pension privatisation, yet it was absent from the Czech reform arena. The Bank's lack of leverage in the Czech Republic coincides with a low level of external debt (see Table 1). For almost a decade now, the only portfolio involved in the Czech pension reform efforts has been the Ministry of Labour and Social Affairs, traditionally inclined towards Bismarckian and Beveridgean paradigms. As the public pension scheme was financially viable without subsidies from the general budget until 1997, it came as no surprise that the Ministry of Finance, a potential intra-governmental advocate of pension privatisation, had no stake in pension reform. However, the Czech pension scheme has been in the red for almost five years now, and successive Finance Ministers have still remained passive. One possible explanation is related to the fact that pension privatisation implies substantial fiscal costs on the short and medium run. On the other hand, the severe economic and financial crisis that hit the Czech Republic in 1997 should be recalled. Given the still shaky bases of the local capital market, the introduction of a mandatory funded tier was deemed particularly inappropriate. Owing to the substantial costs of bank bailouts, the financial sector crisis also translated into a fiscal burden (see World Bank, 2001a), thereby contributing to a narrowing of the budgetary scope for pension privatisation.

The Czech trade unions, another relevant political actor, used to be a fierce critic of the parametric reforms envisaged by the Klaus government. This became particularly manifest during the conflicts surrounding the 1995 Pension Insurance

Act. Even if they were in no position to veto this law, their opposition raised public awareness about the unpopular retrenchment measures and contributed substantially to the electoral defeat of the ruling coalition in 1996. With the appearance of pension privatisation on the Czech agenda, they have changed their stance: instead of pushing for the maintenance of the status quo, they now claim that the existing options to reform the public PAYG scheme have not yet been exhausted in the Czech Republic, opposing a full or partial shift to funding. Given the vociferous role that this set of actors has played in the past, policymakers are likely to take them into account, in spite of the absence of strong corporatist decision making structures in the Czech Republic. Politically, their campaigns translated into support for the Social Democrats and the Pensioners' Party, with the latter single-issue party failing to enter Parliament (see Müller, 1999).

This country's paradigm choice beyond the dominant international mainstream might appear particularly surprising, given the neoliberal discourse of the long-standing Czech Prime Minister, Václav Klaus – seemingly an excellent ideational match for the 'new pension orthodoxy'. However, a closer look reveals that Klaus frequently departed from his 'market economy without an adjective' rhetoric when it came to practical politics (see Kabele and Potůček, 1995; Stark and Bruszt, 1998). It also seems that he never quite warmed up with the idea of *mandating* a funded tier – his favourite pension reform path involved very low replacement rates in the public tier, to create incentives for Czechs to join the supplementary tier voluntarily. In this sense, he may be considered 'too liberal' for the orthodox template. Moreover, Klaus's general coolness towards foreign advisors and the international financial institutions in particular was notorious (see, e.g. Blejer and Coricelli, 1995). Finally, it should also be remembered that since 1996 – i.e. the very moment when the Poles and Hungarians started preparing their partial pension privatisations – Czech governments could not count on a parliamentary majority. In addition, the incoming Social Democrats, traditionally orientated towards a Bismarckian/ Beveridgean-type approach, were opposing pension privatisation, together with their main political ally, the trade unions. Public support for such a paradigm shift was also minimal (Večerník and Matějů, 1999: 201). In the past years the executive's control of the legislature was so limited that the government's plans for a substantial parametric reform were not politically feasible either, thus only increasing their urgency. With elections due in 2002, it is likely to be the next government that will determine the future of the Czech PAYG scheme.

The Slovene case
It was in the mid-1990s that the new orthodox template appeared in the Slovene pension reform arena. According to the account in Stanovnik (this volume), the relevant agenda shifters[24] in the local pension reform debate appear to have been the IMF and the World Bank. During an expert mission to Slovenia in 1995, they emphasised the need for more fundamental reforms in the public pension scheme and also proposed the introduction of a multipillar scheme. Subsequently, the World Bank sought to support pension privatisation in Slovenia by means of an earmarked loan, co-sponsoring an international pension conference in October 1997 and a workshop on second-pillar issues in March 1998, both in Ljubljana, as well as trips to Switzerland and the Netherlands for first-hand experiences with multipillar schemes.

As regards local actors, the push towards a multipillar-type reform came from Tone Rop, a leading figure in the LDS and clearly one of the most influential individual policymakers in Slovenia. When he assumed the Ministry of Labour after the resignation of his social democratic predecessor in 1996, pension reform became the economist's top priority. The initial policy document, elaborated with a significant input of Milan Vodopivec, a former World Bank official, strongly advocated partial pension privatisation. The subsequent White Paper on Pension Reform was co-authored by a team of Phare consultants, among them a leading ILO specialist. These French and Italian social security experts took a more cautious stance on the proposed mandatory second tier, notably with regard to its fiscal implications, a concern corroborated by simulation exercises. However, the final version of the White Paper, published in November 1997, still included pension privatisation.

When the White Paper was discussed with social partners in a working group in January 1998, the Slovene trade unions used this pivotal chance to veto pension privatisation irrevocably. Soon thereafter, they held several large rallies against some of the envisaged parametric reforms and the introduction of a mandatory second tier. Another ally within the 'grey lobby' and a member of the governing coalition during the pension reform process, the Pensioners' Party, also declared its opposition. Moreover, criticism against the government's plan to partially

---

[24] Jacoby (1998:18) has defined agenda shifting as the power to intervene at critical moments, introducing crucial new models in a policy arena.

privatise old-age security was raised by some well-known social security experts with a background in economics and law. One of the most influential Slovene economists, Velimir Bole, highlighted the substantial fiscal costs of the proposed multipillar scheme in a paper commissioned by the World Bank. At this point, the Minister of Finance, Mitja Gaspari, publicly declared that a mandatory second tier would not be fiscally feasible.[25] Subsequently, Tone Rop gave up on pension privatisation. At a cabinet meeting four weeks later, the pension reform course was quietly changed. The draft law on pension and disability insurance, approved by the Slovene government in June 1998, proposed a reform of the public PAYG scheme in combination with the introduction of a voluntary funded tier. After lengthy negotiations within the ruling coalition and with social partners, this law was passed in December 1999. With a rather broad political alliance governing Slovenia from 1997 to 2000, policymaking was characterised by the search for consensus rather than by the rapid enforcement of radical structural reforms.

A comparative discussion of policy choices
The pension policy pursued in the Czech Republic and Slovenia can be interpreted as a move towards the Continental European mainstream in old-age security[26] and as a conscious decision against the policy recommendations of the 'new pension orthodoxy'. It should be noted that in Slovenia it is widely felt that pension reform has been completed with the 1999 reform, yet the opposite is true in the Czech Republic: while virtually all policymakers agree that further reform steps are indispensable, no political consensus has so far been achieved on their nature. The obstacles to parametric pension reform the Czech Republic highlight the potential that such reforms may hold to engender sizeable blame. It is widely observed that parametric reforms, although moderate in the light of paradigmatic alternatives, are politically sensitive. They easily allow the identification of individual losses and are perceived as a mere cutback of acquired entitlements – without anything in exchange (see Holzmann, 1994; Müller, 1999). The above case studies have shown that Czech and Slovene policymakers resorted to strategies of obfuscation, compensation and bundling to reduce political opposition to

---

[25] At this moment, public finances in Slovenia had gone into the red (see Table 1).

[26] Admittedly, old-age security schemes in Continental Europe are extremely diverse. Reference to the 'mainstream' denotes a combination of a public mandatory PAYG scheme, inspired by Bismarckian principles, and a supplementary private tier on a voluntary basis.

their retrenchment policies (see Mácha and Stanovnik, this volume). In the following, the actor-related and structural-institutional factors accounting for the absence of radical pension reform in both transition countries will be identified.

Whereas Ministries of Welfare are traditionally inclined towards the Bismarckian and Beveridgean paradigms and Ministries of Finance have tended to join the ranks of the 'new pension orthodoxy' in many countries, these ideational distinctions proved to be less clear-cut in the two countries analysed here. The unusual degree of mobility between both of these crucial portfolios only indicates that it is harder to attach a specific policy preference to either Ministry in the above country cases: in Slovenia, Tone Rop – the principal advocate of the proposal to partially privatise old-age security – was appointed Minister of Labour after having worked as State Secretary of Privatisation and before becoming Minister of Finance. In the Czech Republic, Jiří Rusnok, a former advisor to the trade union federation, was recently appointed Minister of Finance after having served as Deputy Minister of Labour (see Mácha and Stanovnik, this volume).

It is this context that sheds light on the unusual fact that the Slovene Minister of Labour was the main driving force behind the preparations for partial pension privatisation, and that it was the Minister of Finance who vetoed it. While the essence of the latter is a well-known mechanism, stemming from the relative weight of both portfolios in cabinet, it is at odds with the pattern of several recent pension reforms in Eastern Europe. Most notably, the policy implications are reversed, as pension privatisation was effectively stopped. In the Czech Republic the Ministry of Labour remained in charge of the reform of old-age security, even after fiscal difficulties appeared. Moreover, no prominent policymaker was committed to pension privatisation, and it was only during Tošovský's brief caretaker government that a multipillar scheme was seriously considered. In the midst of political and economic crisis, this was also the only moment when the Czech Ministry of Finance abandoned its passive role, that had first been induced by the pension scheme's surplus and then by concerns regarding high transition costs.

The cases of the Czech Republic and Slovenia show that there is a flip side to the economic factors and considerations that potently pushed pension privatisation elsewhere. In both countries, policymakers were fully aware that pension privatisation would have resulted in substantial fiscal costs[27] in the short

---

[27] See Mesa-Lago (2000) for a comprehensive analysis of transition costs in Latin American pension privatisation.

and medium run, thus complicating future compliance with the Maastricht criteria.[28] Particularly in a context of high implicit pension debt, such as in Slovenia and the Czech Republic, this concern may render Ministers of Finance potentially ambivalent allies of the 'new pension orthodoxy'. Moreover, while the development of the local capital market was a frequently mentioned motive for pension privatisation elsewhere, policymakers in the two countries reviewed here explicitly pointed to the nascent stage of Slovenia's capital market and the crisis-ridden financial sector in the Czech Republic when cautioning against radical pension privatisation. It should be noted that perceiving poor capital market development as a constraint to the introduction of a mandatory funded tier is rare among post-socialist pension reformers. The public's deep-rooted mistrust of the existing financial institutions limited the scope of individually fully-funded old-age provision (see, e.g., Večerník, 2001). Instead of perceiving this as a case for mandating a second tier, Czech and Slovene policymakers decided to give employers more room in the supplementary private schemes.

Trade unions and pensioners' parties also had a role to play in both pension reforms. While this 'grey lobby' strongly resisted parametric changes to the existing PAYG schemes in many transition countries, in the Czech Republic and Slovenia plans to reform old-age security triggered the largest political rallies since independence. The Pensioners' Party failed to enter Parliament in the Czech Republic, yet it even formed part of the governing coalition in Slovenia at the time of the 1999 reform. Even if it could count only on five seats in Parliament, its interests had to be balanced against other policy preferences. In the post-socialist world, the trade unions have also been dubbed 'pensioners' parties' since many of their members are retired. It is interesting to note that neither the Czech nor the Slovene unions were interested in reaping economic benefits from the setting up of their own pension fund in a mandatory tier, contrary to a part of organised labour elsewhere (e.g. in Croatia, Bulgaria and Poland, but also in Argentina and Chile). The Slovene unions were in close contact with their German counterparts, staunch opponents of pension privatisation. In the case of the Czech unions, their

---

[28] The Maastricht criteria imply a commitment to fiscal discipline and price stability in the euro-zone: the government deficit should not exceed 3 percent of GDP, the ratio of government debt to GDP should be 60 percent or lower, and the rate of inflation should not exceed by more than 1.5 percentage points that of the three best-performing EU Member States.

reluctance may be connected with the fact that their early involvement within the voluntary funded tier remained unsuccessful.

The Czech unions voiced strong opposition against the 1995 pension reform law, but started to advocate parametric reforms when pension privatisation appeared on the political agenda. Local decision making structures fail to grant social partners formal veto opportunities (see Casale, 1999), yet Czech policymakers are certainly not keen to revive their vociferous protests. Slovene trade unions enjoyed more voice in the pension reform arena than their Czech counterparts. The existence of formal tripartite structures – the Economic and Social Council, a de facto veto point in Slovene legislation – allowed them to play a significant role in pensions-related decisionmaking. They were invited to discuss subsequent pension reform proposals in tripartite working groups, expressing their adamant opposition to the privatisation of old-age security and contributing significantly to the demise of the multipillar approach in Slovenia. In both the Czech Republic and Slovenia, trade unions were close political allies of the Social Democrats, another important opponent of a mandatory funded pension tier.

Finally, the cases of the Czech Republic and Slovenia indicate that the dynamics of the 'global politics of attention' (Orenstein, 2001; Orenstein and Haas, 2001) need careful differentiation. While international financial institutions, particularly the World Bank, turned into powerful actors in the post-socialist pension reform arena, their leeway as advocates of multipillar schemes is clearly constrained by contextual factors. As illustrated above, Slovenia and the Czech Republic are very advanced transition countries, characterised by a low level of external debt. In this context, both the potential leverage and the interest of the international financial institutions to spend resources on the promotion of pension privatisation is severely limited. As noted, Slovenia – now a high income economy – is even in the process of graduating from World Bank assistance altogether. On the eve of EU accession, both countries showed a strong orientation towards the Continental European mainstream, that EU-sponsored programmes like Phare helped to transmit. Notably in Slovenia, the Phare team featuring Giovanni Tamburi, a long-standing director of the ILO social security department, had a strong impact and helped to shift the balance towards a more critical assessment of funded proposals. Overall, these findings indicate that there may be some potential for diversity in post-socialist pension reform after all. It can only be hoped that this leeway to move beyond the orthodox templates will also help to encourage more pluralism in pensions-related policy advice.

References

Adler, Emanuel/Haas, Peter M. (1992): Conclusion: epistemic communities, world order, and the creation of a reflective research program, *International Organization*, 46 (1), 367–390.
Amerini, Giuliano (2001): Social protection: expenditure on pensions, *Statistics in focus. Population and Living Conditions*, Theme 3, 9/2001, 1–7.
Barr, Nicholas (2000): Reforming Pensions: Myths, Truths, and Policy Choices. IMF Working Paper WP/007139, Washington, DC: IMF.
Beattie, Roger/McGillivray, Warren (1995): A Risky Strategy: Reflections on the World Bank Report 'Averting the Old Age Crisis', *International Social Security Review*, 48 (3–4), 5–22.
Blejer, Mario I./Coricelli, Fabrizio (1995): The Making of Economic Reform in Eastern Europe. Conversations with Leading Reformers in Poland, Hungary and the Czech Republic. Aldershot & Brookfield: Edward Elgar.
Bönker, Frank (2001): Staatseinnahmen und staatliche Handlungsfähigkeit in den osteuropäischen Transformationsländern. Paper presented at the FIT Conference 'The EU Eastern Enlargement as a Milestone of Institutional Change in Eastern Europe', Frankfurt (Oder), October 11–12, 2001.
Brooks, Sarah (1998): Social Protection in a Global Economy: The Case of Pension Reform in Latin America. Duke University, mimeo.
Brooks, Sarah (2001): The diffusion of pension privatization over time and space. Paper prepared for the 2001 Annual Meeting of the American Political Science Association, San Francisco CA, August 30 – September 2, 2001.
Busquets, José Miguel (2001): Análisis comparado de 8 casos de reforma estructural de la Seguridad Social en América Latina (1981–1995). Paper prepared for the 2001 Meeting of the Latin American Studies Association, Washington DC, September 6–8, 2001.
Cain, Michael J. G. (2000): Globalising Tendencies in Public Policy, *EMERGO*, 7 (2), 6–19.
Casale, Giuseppe (ed.) (1999): Social Dialogue in Central and Eastern Europe. Budapest: ILO-CEET.
Cashu, Ilean (2000a): The New Politics of Pension Retrenchment in Russia. Paper prepared for the 2000 National Convention of the American Association for the Advancement of Slavic Studies, Denver CO, November 9–12, 2000.
Cashu, Ilean (2000b): The Politics and Policy Trade-offs of Reforming the Public

Pension System in Post-communist Moldova, *Europe-Asia Studies*, 52 (4), 741–757.

Charlton, Roger/McKinnon, Roddy (2001): Pensions *in* Development. Aldershot et al.: Ashgate.

Chiappe, Rosa (2001): Pension Reform in Bulgaria. In: OECD (ed.): OECD Private Pensions Conference 2000. Private Pensions Series No. 3. Paris: OECD, 43–63.

Chłoń, Agnieszka/Mora, Marek (2001): Pension reforms: What stays behind them? Paper prepared for the joint IIASA World Bank Workshop on 'The Political Economy of Pension Reform', Laxenburg, 5 April 2001.

Corsetti, Giancarlo/Schmidt-Hebbel, Klaus (1997): Pension Reform and Growth. In: Valdés-Prieto, Salvador (ed.): The Economics of Pensions. Principles, Policies, and International Experience. Cambridge, UK: Cambridge University Press, 127–159.

De Deken, Johan Jeroen (1994): Social Policy in Postwar Czechoslovakia. The Development of Old-Age Pensions and Housing Policies During the Period 1945–1989. EUI Working Paper SPS 94/13, Florence: European University Institute.

Dolowitz, David P./Marsh, David (2000): Learning from Abroad: The Role of Policy Transfer in Contemporary Policy-Making, *Governance: An International Journal of Policy and Administration*, 13 (1), 5–24.

Drazen, Allan (2000): Political Economy in Macroeconomics. Princeton NJ: Princeton University Press.

Drazen, Allan/Grilli, Vittorio (1993): The Benefit of Crises for Economic Reforms, *American Economic Review*, 83 (3), 598–607.

EBRD (2001a): EBRD Annual Report 2000. http://www.ebrd.com/english/public/index.htm

EBRD (2001b): Czech Republic – Investment Profile 2001. London: European Bank for Reconstruction and Development.

EBRD (2001c): Slovenia – Investment Profile 2001. London: European Bank for Reconstruction and Development.

Eurostat (2001): Demographic Consequences for the EU of the Accession of Twelve Candidate Countries, *Statistics in focus. Population and Social Conditions*, Theme 3, 12/2001, 1–7.

Fultz, Elaine/Ruck, Markus (2000): Pension Reform in Central and Eastern Europe: An Update on the Restructuring of National Pension Schemes in Selected Countries. ILO-CEET Report No. 25. Budapest: ILO-CEET.

Gesell-Schmidt, Rainer/Müller, Katharina/Süß, Dirck (1999): Social Security Reform and Privatisation in Poland: Parallel Projects or Integrated Agenda? *Osteuropa-Wirtschaft*, 44 (4), 428–450.

Haas, Peter M. (1992): Introduction: epistemic communities and international policy coordination, *International Organization*, 46 (1), 1–35.

Harberger, Arnold C. (1993): Secrets of Success: A Handful of Heroes, *American Economic Review – Papers and Proceedings*, 83 (2), 342–350.

Hartl, Jan/Večerník, Jiří (1992): Economy, Policy and Welfare in Transition. In: Ferge, Zsuzsa/Kolberg, Jon Eivind (eds): Social Policy in a Changing Europe. Frankfurt/Main: Campus, & Boulder, CO: WestviewPress, 161–175.

Hellman, Joel S./Jones, Geraint/Kaufmann, Daniel (2000): 'Seize the State, Seize the Day'. State Capture, Corruption, and Influence in Transition. World Bank Policy Research Working Paper No. 2444. Washington DC: World Bank.

Hellman, Joel S./Kaufmann, Daniel (2001): Confronting the Challenges of State Capture in Transition Economies, *Finance and Development*, 38 (3). http://www.imf.org/external/pubs/ft/fandd/

Hirschman, Albert O. (1991): The Rhetoric of Reaction: Perversity, Futility, Jeopardy. Cambridge, MA: Harvard University Press.

Huber, Evelyne/Stephens, John D. (2000): The Political Economy of Pension Reform: Latin America in Comparative Perspective. UNRISD Occasional Paper 7, Geneva: UNRISD.

Immergut, Ellen M. (1992): Health Politics – Interests and Institutions in Western Europe. Cambridge, UK: Cambridge University Press.

Isuani, Ernesto Aldo/San Martino, Jorge A. (1995): El nuevo sistema previsional argentino ¿Punto final a una larga crisis? Primera parte: *Boletín Informativo Techint*, 281, 41–56; Segunda parte: *Boletín Informativo Techint*, 282, 43–67.

Jacoby, Wade (1998): Talking the Talk: The Cultural and Institutional Effects of Western Models. Paper prepared for the Conference 'Postcommunist Transformation and the Social Sciences. Cross-Disciplinary Approaches', Berlin, October 30–31, 1998.

James, Estelle (1996): Protecting the Old and Promoting Growth. A Defense of 'Averting the Old Age Crisis'. Policy Research Working Paper No. 1570. Washington, DC: World Bank.

James, Estelle/Brooks, Sarah (2001): The Political Economy of Structural Pension Reform. In: Holzmann, Robert/Stiglitz, Joseph E. (eds): New Ideas about Old

Age Security. Toward Sustainable Pension Systems in the 21st Century. Washington, DC: The World Bank, 133–170.

Jelínek, Tomáš and Ondřej Schneider (1997a): Pension System Reform in the Czech Republic – Liberální Institut Project Proposal. Prague, mimeo.

Jelínek, Tomáš and Ondřej Schneider (1997b): Time for Pension Reform in the Czech Republic', *Transitions*, 4 (1), 77–81.

Kabele, Jiří/Potůček, Martin (1995): The Formation and Implementation of Social Policy in the Czech Republic as a Political Process. Research Paper No. 5. Prague: START.

Kay, Stephen J. (1998): Politics and Social Security Reform in the Southern Cone and Brazil. PhD Dissertation, University of California at Los Angeles, mimeo.

Kay, Stephen J. (1999): Unexpected Privatizations. Politics and Social Security Reforms in the Southern Cone, *Comparative Politics*, 31 (4), 403–422.

Kornai, János (1997): Reforming the Welfare State in Postsocialist Societies, *World Development*, 25 (8), 1183–1186.

Krueger, Anne O. (ed.) (2000): Economic Policy Reform. The Second Stage. Chicago & London: The University of Chicago Press.

Laursen, Thomas (2000): Pension System Viability and Reform Alternatives in the Czech Republic. Working Paper WP/00/16. Washington DC: IMF.

Lo Vuolo, Rubén M. (1996): Reformas previsionales en América Latina: el caso argentino, *Comercio Exterior*, 46 (9), 692–702.

Madrid, Raúl (1998): The Determinants of Pension Reform Around the World, 1992–97. Paper prepared for the 1998 Annual Meeting of the American Political Science Association, Boston MA, September 3–6, 1998.

Madrid, Raúl (1999): The New Logic of Social Security Reform: Politics and Pension Privatization in Latin America. PhD Dissertation, Stanford University, mimeo.

Madrid, Raúl (2001): Retiring the State: The Politics of Pension Privatization. Book manuscript, University of Texas at Austin, mimeo.

Madrid, Raúl (2002): The Politics (and Economics) of Pension Privatization in Latin America, forthcoming in: *Latin American Research Review*, 37 (2), Spring 2002.

Mesa-Lago, Carmelo (1996): Pension system reforms in Latin America: the position of the international organizations, *CEPAL Review*, (60), 73–98.

Mesa-Lago, Carmelo (1998): Comparative Features and Performance of Structural Pension Reforms in Latin America, *Brooklyn Law Review*, 64 (3), 771–793.

Mesa-Lago, Carmelo (1999): Política y reforma de la seguridad social en América Latina, *Nueva Sociedad* (160), Marzo-Abril 1999, 133–150.

Mesa-Lago, Carmelo (2000): Estudio comparativo de los costos fiscales en la transición de ocho reformas de pensiones en América Latina. Serie Financiamiento del Desarrollo 93. Santiago de Chile: CEPAL.

Mesa-Lago, Carmelo/Müller, Katharina (2002): The Politics of Pension Reform in Latin America, forthcoming in: *Journal of Latin American Studies*.

Mayntz, Renate/Scharpf, Fritz W. (1995): Der Ansatz des akteurzentrierten Institutionalismus. In: Mayntz, Renate/Scharpf, Fritz W. (eds): Gesellschaftliche Selbstregelung und politische Steuerung. Frankfurt/Main & New York: Campus, 39–72.

Mora, Marek (1999): The Political Economy of Pension Reforms: The Case of Latin America. Washington DC, mimeo.

Müller, Katharina (1999): The Political Economy of Pension Reform in Central-Eastern Europe. Cheltenham & Northampton MA: Edward Elgar.

Müller, Katharina (2001): The Making of Pension Privatisation in Latin America and Eastern Europe – A Cross-Regional Comparison. Paper presented at the joint IIASA World Bank Workshop on 'The Political Economy of Pension Reform', Laxenburg, 5 April 2001.

Müller, Katharina (2002): Pension Reform Paths in Central-Eastern Europe and the Former Soviet Union, forthcoming in: *Social Policy and Administration*, 36 (2).

Nelson, Joan M. (2001): The Politics of Pension and Health-Care Reforms in Hungary and Poland. In: Kornai, János/Haggard, Stephan/Kaufman, Robert R. (eds): Reforming the State. Fiscal and Welfare Reform in Post-Socialist Countries. Cambridge, UK: Cambridge University Press, 235–266.

Ney, Steven (2000): Are You Sitting Comfortably... Then We'll Begin: Three Gripping Policy Stories About Pension Reform, *Innovation: The European Journal of Social Sciences*, 13 (4), 341–371.

Nikolov, Nikolay (2001): Pension Companies and Funds – Current Stage and Possible Trends. In: Bulgarian Pension Reform Project (ed.): The Bulgarian Pension Model One Year after the Start. Sofia: USAID, 18–20.

Offe, Claus (1994): Der Tunnel am Ende des Lichts. Erkundungen der politischen Transformation im Neuen Osten. Frankfurt/Main & New York: Campus.

Orenstein, Mitchell (2000): How Politics and Institutions Affect Pension Reform in Three Postcommunist Countries. World Bank Policy Research Working Paper 2310, Washington DC.

Orenstein, Mitchell (2001): Mapping the Diffusion of Pension Innovation. Paper prepared for the 2001 Annual Meeting of the American Political Science Association, San Francisco CA, August 30 – September 2, 2001.

Orenstein, Mitchell/Haas, Martine (2001): The Global Politics of Attention and Social Policy Transformation in East-Central Europe. Forthcoming in a volume edited by Miguel Glatzer and Dietrich Rueschemeyer.

Orszag, Peter R./Stiglitz, Joseph E. (2001): Rethinking Pension Reform: Ten Myths About Social Security Systems. In: Holzmann, Robert/Stiglitz, Joseph E. (eds): New Ideas about Old Age Security. Toward Sustainable Pension Systems in the 21st Century. Washington, DC: The World Bank, 17–62.

Pierson, Paul (1996): The New Politics of the Welfare State, *World Politics*, 48 (2), 143–179.

Pierson, Paul/Weaver, R. Kent (1993): Imposing Losses in Pension Policy. In: Weaver, R. Kent/Rockman, Bert A. (eds.): Do Institutions Matter? Government Capabilities in the United States and Abroad. Washington DC: The Brookings Institution, 110–150.

Rodrik, Dani (1996): Understanding Economic Policy Reform, *Journal of Economic Literature*, XXXIV (March 1996), 9–41.

Rodrik, Dani (1998): Promises, Promises: Credible Policy Reform via Signalling. In: Sturzenegger, Federico/Tommasi, Mariano (eds): The Political Economy of Reform. Cambridge, MA & London: MIT Press, 307–327.

Sachs, Jeffrey (1994): Life in the Economic Emergency Room. In: Williamson, John (ed.): The Political Economy of Policy Reform: Washington DC: Institute for International Economics, 503–523.

Scharpf, Fritz W. (1997): Games Real Actors Play: Actor-Centered Institutionalism in Policy Research. Boulder CO: WestviewPress.

Schneider, Ondřej (1996a): Pension Reform in the Czech Republic: Gradualistic Czechs, *Central European Banker*, (December 1996), 22–26.

Schneider, OndYej (1996b): The Reform of the Czech Pension System – Proposals and Qualifications. Paper prepared for the Conference 'Social Security Systems – A Threat to Public Finances?', Warsaw, November 14–15, 1996.

Stapel, Silke (2001): The GDP of the Candidate Countries. Annual GDP, growth rates and main aggregates, *Statistics in focus. Economy and Finance*, Theme 2, 28/2001, 1–7.

Stark, David/Bruszt, László (1998): Postsocialist Pathways – Transforming Politics and Property in East Central Europe: Budapest: Central European University Press.

Stiglitz, Joseph E. (1998): An Agenda for Development in the Twenty-First Century. In: Pleskovic, Boris/Stiglitz, Joseph E. (eds): Annual World Bank Conference on Development Economics 1997. Washington, DC: The World Bank, 17–31.

Sturzenegger, Federico/Tommasi, Mariano (eds) (1998): The Political Economy of Reform. Cambridge, MA & London: MIT Press.

Tommasi, Mariano/Velasco, Andrés (1996): Where Are We in the Political Economy of Reform? *Journal of Policy Reform*, 1, 187–238.

UNDP (2001): Human Development Report 2001. Making New Technologies Work for Human Development. New York: United Nations Development Programme.

Večerník, Jiří (2001): Pension System in the Czech Republic: From Reform to Non-Reform. Forthcoming in: Kalb, Don/Kovács, János M. (eds): Comparative Institutional Reform in Social Policy. East-Central Europe in a European Context (1989–2001). Vienna: Institut für die Wissenschaften vom Menschen.

Večerník, Jiří/Matějů, Petr (eds) (1999): Ten years of rebuilding capitalism: Czech society after 1989. Prague: Academia.

Weyland, Kurt (2001): Learning from Foreign Models in Latin American Policy Reform. Paper prepared for the 2001 Annual Meeting of the American Political Science Association, San Francisco CA, August 30 – September 2, 2001.

Williamson, John (2000): What Should the World Bank Think about the Washington Consensus? *The World Bank Research Observer*, 15 (2), 251–264.

Williamson, John (ed.) (1994): The Political Economy of Policy Reform. Washington, DC: Institute for International Economics.

Williamson, John (ed.) (1990): Latin American Adjustment: How Much Has Happened? Washington, DC: Institute for International Economics.

Williamson, John and Stephan Haggard (1994): The Political Conditions for Economic Reform. In: Williamson (ed.): The Political Economy of Policy Reform. Washington DC: Institute for International Economics, 525–596.

World Bank (1994): Averting the Old Age Crisis. Policies to Protect the Old and Promote Growth. Washington, DC: Oxford University Press.

World Bank (2000): Republic of Slovenia – Country Assistance Strategy. Progress Report. Washington DC: World Bank.

World Bank (2001a): Czech Republic – Enhancing the Prospects for Growth with

Fiscal Stability. A World Bank Public Expenditure Review. Washington DC: World Bank.

World Bank (2001b): Czech Republic at a Glance. Washington, DC, mimeo.

World Bank (2001c): Slovenia at a Glance. Washington, DC, mimeo.

World Bank (2001d): World Development Report 2000/2001: Attacking Poverty. Oxford et al.: Oxford University Press.

www.ingramcontent.com/pod-product-compliance
Ingram Content Group UK Ltd.
Pitfield, Milton Keynes, MK11 3LW, UK
UKHW021321180426
11947UKWH00015B/1353